It Do Be Like That Sometimes

A College Student's Guide To Living Life
From Some Of The Wisest People in History

by Ryan Taylor

It Do Be Like That Sometimes

A College Student's Guide To Living Life From Some Of The Wisest People in History

Copyright © 2022 by Ryan Taylor

All rights reserved. No part of this book may be reproduced in any form by any electronic or mechanical means including photocopying, recording, or information storage and retrieval without permission in writing from the author.

ISBN-13: 979-8-218-02773-5

Cover art by Ryan Taylor
Edited by Ebook Launch
Interior design by Ryan Taylor

Give feedback on the book at:
itdobelikethatryan@gmail.com

Twitter: @BeLikeThatItDo_

First Edition

Printed in the U.S.A

To my mom and dad, for all your love and guidance.
To Amanda, Carson, and the rest of my family, for your endless support.
To Nana, for the support and guidance every step of the way.

In memory of Jim Birkbeck
A man who had a profound impact on my life.
A great mentor, friend, and grandfather.

INTRODUCTION

Hello,

    I see that you have found this book and are beginning your journey of learning how to become a better person and live a better life. We all have our own personal reasons for embarking to become better. The purpose of this book is to help college-age people become more open to the questions and issues that they will inevitably face while commencing on this new time in their lives. The great thing about all of these quotes is that they can apply to anyone. I write to young adults because I am a young adult, and that is all I know how to do so far. Anyone can read this book and gain some perspective and wisdom on their life. In my personal experience, I have seen some of these quotes stick with students in middle school to people well past retirement age. The great thing about this is that you can mentally substitute your own experiences in for the ones that I give, and the wisdom will still solve your problems. There is no age limit on virtue, knowledge, and wisdom. I hope to whomever is reading this that you can take away some of the lessons that are presented in this book and apply them to your own life. At the end of the day, it does not matter if your dreams and ambitions are higher than mine, or if the problems you have are worse. I just hope that you can take these quotes and lessons and use them to help you live the best and fullest life you can.

    —Ryan

Why Should You Listen to What I Have to Say?

At the time of writing this, I am a twenty-one-year-old college student. I attend the University of Kansas, which is the largest public university in my state. I am writing this for me just as much as I am for you. I am going to college during a global pandemic, which has not been easy. I am learning how to become an adult, which has its challenges. I am also going through a breakup, and this book has helped keep my mind off of all the issues that come with that experience. One of my hopes is that this book helps you as much as it has been helping me. I was not an exceptional student coming out of high school. I did not come to this university on a full-ride academic or athletic scholarship; in fact, I came here with few scholarships. So, you might be wondering why you should listen to me. Well, to start, I am just like you. I am at college and understand the grind that comes with it. Once you get to college, you can sympathize with others about school because you know just how bad some weeks can be with work management and stress overload. I have been at college for a few years now, and I like to think that I understand the school and social life conflict. I understand what having bad professors is like. I also like to consider myself a pretty well-rounded guy when it comes to life. This is another reason to listen because I have had the opportunity of doing and being around a little bit of everything. I am not a college athlete, although I have close friends who are, and I have played many sports growing up. I understand the commitment and grind that you have to put in to be successful on the field and in the classroom. I know what it is like to be the lonely freshman as well as the one with a crazy social life. They each have their own unique set of perks and problems. My life experiences have not been boxed into one or two categories; rather, I jump around and have done a little bit of everything. This allows me the unique experiences of knowing what many people are going through. If I cannot give a firsthand account of what they are going through, I can at least sympathize with them because I know, based on my similar experiences, what it must be like. No, I cannot say that I have done every single thing that you, the person reading this, has done. I like to think that I have done and seen enough that I can give you a broad concept or idea, and you can relate it to something more personal. So that is why I think that you should listen to what I have to say. I may be young for someone to think I have wisdom, but you would be surprised at how much college-age people know. So, who knows, you might just learn something from me.

What You Should Know Before Reading

I chose these quotes based on my criteria. First, it was whether or not these quotes spoke to me. If I felt like a certain quote pertained to something in my life, I put it in there. These quotes come from some of the most knowing people who have ever lived. From ancient stoics to America's founding fathers, this book offers a wide range of wisdom from some pretty cool people. I also have some quotes from religious texts. I think that regardless of what your religion is, you can still learn something from all religious books. I find it wrong to not even acknowledge some of the wisdom that others can give just because you have a different view on something. I do not know what your religious stance is, but I hope that you can at least look at other religious texts with an open mind to understand the moral behind the quote and think about if you could apply that to your life. I did not put anything of huge controversy in here so there is no need to freak out. This is just more a heads up that there are multiple different religious passages that found their way into this book. Some of the people who I have quoted have controversial backgrounds. I understand that what these people did should not be idolized. One example is that there are a few quotes from Thomas Jefferson in this book. For a man who said, "All men are created equal," he sure had a lot of slaves. I do not agree with many of his life choices. I also think that while he did some bad things, he also did some good things, and he had some good quotes. Just because I put their quotes in this book does not mean that I expect you to embody everything that they did in life. Just as it is possible for a good man to do bad, I think a bad man can do good. The good in this case was publishing some quotes that are worth reading and living by.

Last Thing, I Pinky Promise

This is the last thing, I promise. There is a certain way I recommend you read this book. I wrote this book to be read one page a day, like a devotional. I know that you are all very busy people, so I do not expect you to have time to sit down and read for hours every day. This is why I want to give you something to think about after about one minute of reading. It is my hope that if you read one page every day, you will go throughout your own life with a little more knowledge and wisdom from the last day. That being said, if you want to read this book straight through, I cannot stop you. What I will warn you is that if you read it straight through, you might find some crossover from one page to the next. The ideas and principles in this book are not vast, but rather a few ideas and virtues that I hope you learn to embody. If you decide to read this book straight through, you might think to yourself, "Man, he said basically the same thing a few pages ago." Yeah, that is the point. I think rather than confusing you with new virtues and ideas every single day, it is easier for you to understand and work to embody a few really good ones. Just understand that this book is more of an idea-a-day type of book. Read it a page a day or read it straight through in one day. Either way, the ideas will get through to you. From start to finish, I hope this book opens your eyes to something new and helps you out.

January

January 1st

"The road to paradise begins in hell."
- Dante Alighieri: 13th Century Italian Poet & Writer

College can be a scary and exciting time in your life. You are going to make some major decisions about what you want to do, who you want to be, and try to figure out how you are going to do those things. Maybe it is deciding where you want to go to college or what you want to major in at college. Most of these decisions have to be made before even starting your first college class. No matter what these decisions are, you are looking at an uphill battle to get to the finish line. It is easy to think that you can just show up to college and do nothing and pass in four years. College is not a walk in the park; there will be sleepless nights in a library, failure, and many stressful deadlines. But nothing good comes easy. Whether it is a college diploma or a good grade on a test, you will have to go through some struggles to obtain that. Every big thing that you want will require you to persevere through some hard and uncomfortable times. The bad is what makes the good that much better. Embrace the work of these hardships because it will make reaching the end that much more rewarding.

January 2nd

"Be tolerant with others and strict with yourself."

- Marcus Aurelius: Roman Emperor & Stoic Philosopher

―――――――――――― ◆ ――――――――――――

While you are at college, you will meet and get to know a lot of people. Some of them will become your best friends—others...not so much. You will deal with unreliable classmates who do not help on a group project, or some jerk you have to deal with at a party. Their unreliableness and rudeness are not something you can control. If you are the one who is being unreliable on the group project or a jerk at the party, you have the power to prevent that. You can catch the problem and work to make sure it does not happen again. That is your business, and you need to be strict with yourself to control it. You must learn to accept what you can manage and let others be. The only thing you can control is yourself. What other people decide to do is up to them, not you. You have enough to worry about in college as it is; let other people figure themselves out. Other people are going to make mistakes, and that is something you cannot control. It sucks when other people's mistakes affect you, then be strict with yourself to be better and not make others deal with your mistakes.

January 3rd

"Circumstances don't make the man; they only reveal him to himself."

- Epictetus: Ancient Greek Philosopher

The fact of the matter is that in college, you will have days, weeks, and months that just do not go your way. This is your first exposure to the "real world," and you are trying to go about it for your first time on your own. There will be months when you fail a few tests, your significant other breaks up with you in the middle of the week, and you have to give a big presentation the next morning for a class. These are just times when you will have to buckle down and really dig deep to get through it. You always have a choice when life's circumstances are not going your way. You can either accept these defeats and give up, or you can fight through them and allow yourself to grow. These tough times will allow you to become tougher and grow stronger as a person. It is amazing to look back at yourself after going through some tough times to see how much stronger you are and how much you have grown. No one ever said it was going to be easy, but it will be very rewarding in the end.

January 4th

"Care about what other people think and you will always be their prisoner."

- Lao Tzu: Ancient Chinese Philosopher

College is a time for you to grow and become your own person. This means you get to make new friends and meet new people. It also means that you want to be liked and seen as a favorable person to hang out with. What you cannot do is get too caught up in what other people think of you. Ultimately, what difference does it make if someone likes you or not? You are on a campus of thousands of people, so there is no reason to worry about if someone really likes you. This person has talked to you maybe once, and you are going to let what they think of you based on one encounter worry you? The more you worry about what someone thinks of you, the worse off you are going to make college for yourself. You are letting this one person control how you feel about yourself. Doing this will lead you to live your life trying to be like what someone else wants, rather than what you want. You finally have the chance to be independent, and you are going to spend it trying to make one other person happy? Be your own person and do what you love; that will lead you to happiness.

January 5th

"The greater the obstacle, the more glory in overcoming it."

- Moliere: 17th Century French Playwright

A question to ask yourself is, "Where do I want to go in life?" This is a great question because it challenges you to think in the future and start setting some goals for yourself. It is easy to not want to do anything with your life and just wait around and see what happens. However, is this your ultimate goal in life, to wait around doing nothing? Hopefully, that is not your goal because you are destined for bigger and better things than that. If you have high aspirations and goals for your life, it will not be easy. If your plans were easy, then everyone would do it too. It is time for you to go out and start your journey toward those high places you want to go. It will take some time, and it will not always be easy, but that makes the journey special. You are going to have to work for every bit of it. The amount of work that you put in will make the end feel so much better. So do not ask for any shortcuts to your goals; rather, enjoy the ups and downs of the journey, and you will enjoy the finish line.

January 6th

"He who asks is a fool for five minutes, but he who does not ask remains a fool forever."

- Chinese Proverb

This is a situation you might run into when you are in college. Many colleges require that their students take some sort of foreign language. You want to be different from your friends, so you enroll in Russian. This language is no joke; it is a challenge from the new alphabet to the almost impossible grammar. In the first class you realize you are the only student in the class who was not majoring in Russian studies, and you feel pretty out of place. This means you are always asking questions in order to keep up with everyone. Even though you may not always feel great about asking so many questions, you will look back and be glad you did. You are not going to get better at the grammar or the speaking without the numerous questions. Sure, you may feel like an idiot after asking a few questions, but imagine how much more idiotic you would feel for missing a question on a test or assignment over something you could have just asked a question over.

January 7th

"Luck is what happens when preparation meets opportunity."

- Lucius Annaeus Seneca: Roman Stoic Philosopher

When you go to college, you will find it hard not to notice how some people tend to just be lucky. For whatever reason it may be, here are some ways on how you, too, can obtain some of this luck. Some people will call you lucky, but they do not see the preparation you put into it. When you get the top grade on the exam, and the professor congratulates you, it is almost certain that someone will come up and say, "What did you do to get so lucky?" These people do not see the countless hours you spent alone studying the material for the exam. They also do not see you attending office hours and asking questions to the professor. You have the opportunity for so many things; the work you put into it will determine the "luck" you are given. You prepared for something, and that gets you a bit of luck on your side; what more could you want? No matter what options you have in front of you, give all your effort to prepare, and you will be astonished at how well you come out. Maybe it is luck, or perhaps you were the most prepared to accomplish your goal.

January 8th

"Anger is a bad counselor."
— *French Proverb*

Think about this: you are taking the final exam for a logic course. It is not a long test, around six questions. These questions, however, have about twenty steps to them. You work all the logical equations out except for the last one. You really need to pass this final to do well in this class. It is a timed final, and you feel the seconds ticking away. The pressure from both the time and need to do good on this exam is starting to get to you. Frustration is rising because you cannot figure out how to solve this one problem. That frustration starts to turn to anger. You think, how can I be so stupid to not figure this one problem out? The rage and pressure are clouding your thoughts, so it is no real surprise that you cannot figure this problem out. You close your eyes, take a deep breath, and give yourself a few seconds to relax. When you are calmer, the answer hits you and you finish the problem. Anger, frustration, and pressure can cloud our minds and cause us to not see things clearly. When you rid yourself of these feelings, it allows you to see clearly and realize how simple your problem actually was.

January 9th

"Be patient and tough; someday this pain will be useful to you."

- Ovid: Ancient Roman Poet

Painful moments are bound to happen to you. You are going to get heartbroken, sometimes pretty badly. It is awful, and you feel like your life is over. How could you ever find another person like them? Well, here is some advice; your life is not over, and you will find someone better than them. There are other people out there who are more deserving of you than your ex was. These new possible relationships will allow you to be yourself and find true happiness. It will hurt, but you need to think about why your last relationship did not work. There will be some dark thoughts and tears, but if you can find the lesson from the relationship, that is all you need to remember. Your ex is gone, and that is the past. Use what you learned from that relationship in future relationships so the same problem does not happen again. The pain you feel hurts now, but someday it will leave. You will have learned a valuable lesson from that failed relationship. You can use that for future ones to have better success. Someday the pain will get better, and you will be able to use those painful lessons for future situations.

January 10th

"Do not fear mistakes. You will know failure. Continue to reach out."

- Benjamin Franklin: 18th Century Writer & Inventor

Sure, things will happen, and you wish they had played out differently. You bombed a big test, you got rejected at the bar, your groupmates did not help on the group project, or you lost your job. These are all times of defeat in your life. You will probably end up in bed wondering about what you could have done differently. It sucks to go through defeats. They are not pleasant. These defeats are not signs that you have a flawed character, rather, that you may have made one poor decision. Just because you made a bad decision does not mean that you are a bad person. You will go through plenty of defeats in college, but that does not mean you are a failure; rather, you were unable to make an appropriate judgment of a situation. You probably should have studied more for that test or cleaned yourself up before you approached someone in the bar or tried to contact your groupmates for the project. Just because you messed up and failed at something does not mean you are a failure; it just means you are learning, and is that not why you went to college?

January 11th

"If it's endurable, then endure it. Stop complaining."
- Marcus Aurelius: Roman Emperor & Stoic Philosopher

It is easy to sit around and complain about everything you have going on in your life. Between exams, social schedule, internships, and whatever else you have going on, it is easy to get swallowed up by all the new responsibilities in your life. College is the first time you are finally on your own, and it does not really hit you that you will have to deal with these new issues. There will be plenty of times in your college career when you are so overwhelmed with all that you have going on that you complain about it to your friends or family. You need to realize that this is your college career, not anyone else's. You need to stop complaining and just do what you have to. You will realize that you are much tougher than you first thought. You will manage to get through your exams and keep your social life. We are all much more resilient than we think we are. While our responsibilities might seem overwhelming, they are usually achievable. Stop complaining and just do what needs to be done; you will be surprised how easy it was to overcome those obstacles.

January 12th

"They lose the day in expectation of the night, and the night in fear of the dawn."

- Lucius Annaeus Seneca: Roman Stoic Philosopher

◆

This is a reminder to not ever get too far ahead of yourself. It is good to keep up your future goals and to think ahead, but constantly living in the future means missing the present. Live in the now and enjoy what is here right before you. If you spend all your time worrying and thinking of the future, you never have the pleasure of experiencing the present. Pushing events that could be done now into the future has only taken them away from the now. Enjoy everything right now. It is a gift to experience everything as you can. It also does not have to be in fear. It can also be in anticipation. There will be times when you are so excited for something in the future that you wish away the present. Think about how many hours and even days you lose when you look forward to something in the future. It is okay to be excited about something to come, but do not completely throw away the present because of it. Learn to enjoy everything now, and then when the thing in the future finally comes around, you can enjoy it.

January 13th

"Happiness is the feeling that power increases – that resistance is being overcome."

- Friedrich Nietzsche: 19th Century German Philosopher

What is the reason that you are unhappy? Oftentimes, we understand that we are unhappy, but we struggle to find the answer to where the unhappiness comes from. You might be disappointed because you feel that you have not completed something you really want to. The lack of accomplishment is often why many people are not happy. Whatever you have not accomplished, it is time to start. We all know that euphoric feeling when we complete a goal. It is arguably one of the best feelings in the world. This is a high that you can constantly chase. You have an uncompleted plan, you chase after it, you complete it, you feel good, you find the next dream, and start the process all over again. Not only do you get to constantly chase the feeling of success that makes you happy, but you are also continually improving at something you can look back at and be proud of. There is no real downside to accomplishing goals and finding the new goals to achieve. You will be filled with happiness and accomplishment.

January 14th

"Do not be afraid of greatness. Some are born great, some achieve greatness and others have greatness cast upon them."

- William Shakespeare: 16th Century English Playwright & Poet

---

It is hard to accept change sometimes. We might live a good life right now, but what if you could live a great life? You might be a good student, have good friends, and even have a decent relationship. This good life is fine, but think about having a great life. Instead of a good student, you could be a great student. Rather than just having good friends, you could have great friends. Maybe you feel that things might not be perfect in your personal relationships. Still, you are willing to stay where you are because it is familiar. Just because you are in an auspicious place now does not mean that this is where you are meant to be forever. Think about what you have right now; could it be better? Is your partner using you or helping you aspire to be the best version of you? It is not always easy to figure these questions out, but they are necessary. It is not comfortable seeking out a great life, but you will be glad that you did not settle for the good life once you find it.

January 15th

"If you wait for perfect conditions, you will never get anything done."

- Ecclesiastes 11:4

We all have goals we want to get done. You probably have a handful of long-term goals and many short-term goals. Each and every one of these goals is obtainable to you. You are probably looking at those short-term goals first, perhaps just getting some homework done in college. After several weeks of a wearying school schedule, accomplishing even the simplest tasks can get pretty hard. You can sit there and talk with your friends about the massive amount of homework you have to finish this week. Sure, it feels good to complain about it to someone, but that does not help the task get done. You need to stop talking to your friends and just start on your homework. The only way it will get done is if you start working on it. If you think to wait for a perfect time to start, then you will never find it. Yes, it will probably not be the most fun thing you will ever do, but just think, the sooner you start, the sooner you finish. The easy option might be to procrastinate your work, but that will eventually hurt you more than helping. Start the job, and it will get done.

January 16th

"He that does good to others does good to himself."

- Lucius Annaeus Seneca: Roman Stoic Philosopher

It is no surprise that we feel satisfaction when we help others out. We should always be open to helping others. It can be big, like donating money or time to a charitable cause. Or it could be something small like holding a door for someone. No matter what you are doing, you should try to do it out of the goodness of your character. Because when you do good deeds, it comes back around to you. Sometimes it is in the form of a good deed returned. You may have noticed that when you help someone out, it is usually pretty easy for them to return the favor when you need a hand. You should not expect something in return from others; just do it because it feels good to help. Sometimes a reward will come in the form of the good feeling of helping someone out. It is nice to walk away from a situation and smile, knowing that you could help someone out today. Your character is defined by what you do. If you do good, then your character will be good. Be good to others, and that goodness will reflect on you.

January 17th

"Words kill, words give life; they're either poison or fruit – You choose."

- King Solomon: Biblical King

Can you think back to what someone said to you that you will never forget? Either what they said was so good that you could never forget it, or it was so hurtful that you could not forget it. Is it not amazing that you can still remember what that person said to you after so long, good or bad? Now, think about the person who said that phrase that you cannot forget. Chances are that if they said something good, you probably think of them as a good person. If they said something hurtful, you probably do not see them as great people. Now, think about all phrases and words you have spoken to others. They make the same memories as you, both good and bad. What you say to other people sticks with them, even if you have forgotten. Do you want the words that stick with others to be good? Do you want them to think of what you said and remember you as a nice person? If you're going to be thought of as a good person, it starts with what you say to others. Speak to them with words of encouragement and kindness, and they will remember you as such.

January 18th

"Glory follows virtue as is it were its shadow."
- *Marcus Tullius Cicero: Roman Statesman & Philosopher*

Have you ever noticed that the more abundance of good deeds you do, the good usually tend to come back to you? The world has a funny way of repaying you for your interest in others. You can probably think of a handful of times you have helped someone for no other reason than just to help and be a good person. Sure enough, within the week, you had something good happen to you. There is no one way to live a virtuous life. Some people do righteous deeds for religious reasons; others do it for the general feeling of doing good for the world. As long as you try to do these virtuous good deeds for the sake of helping others, rather than doing them to get something back, then you will certainly be rewarded for your efforts. As long as you are motivated to do good deeds for someone to positively affect someone else, there will be a reward down the line for you. It might be immediately after you do your act of good virtue, or it could be months later. Just as a shadow gets longer or shorter depending on the day, so is the time that a good deed comes back to repay itself with you.

January 19th

"If a man knew where he would fall, he would spread straw there first."

- Finnish Proverb

You will not be able to plan for every setback, failure, and issue that arises in your life. You will fall down hard sometimes, and it is up to you to get back up. This takes a certain amount of determination and willpower to do. The falls that happen when you do not see the unexpected setback or failure are the worst. They blindside you, and it takes a lot of effort to get back up. You can also learn from these failures and make some fallback plans for the future. If you know something bad might happen, you can plan for that so that you have a cushion to fall back on when something bad does happen. Plan ahead and see the possible issues that could occur in the future will be the difference between you failing and being setback for a while or failing and recovering pretty quickly. You are not always going to have a safety net for every situation in your life. However, if you can have a few cushions to fall back on, that is a lot better than none. You should make a plan and make a backup plan if the first one fails. It is a lot easier and much less painful to recover from.

January 20th

"That which does not kill us makes us stronger."
- Friedrich Nietzsche: 19th Century German Philosopher

Tough times are inevitable for all of us. You are going to go through patches of your life where everything sucks. This is not something you should fear and hide from because it will happen no matter what. Usually, these tough times do not give you the option to fail; they just allow you to be tougher. Sometimes it is not a situation where you fail and are done or succeed and keep going. When your significant other does not work out, that does not mean you have failed at love. This is a situation where you did not fail and are done with love forever; it is just a lesson to learn for later. This is where you as an individual get stronger. No one knows the mental battles you have to go through daily, only you do. And you will fight those battles and come out a tougher and overall better person. Pretty soon, that tough time in your life will pass, and you will feel like a new person. You are wiser and tougher, and you feel like you can take on new challenges. Like all things, this dark time will pass, and as long as you keep going, you will come out a tougher, better person from it.

January 21st

"Iron sharpens iron, and one person sharpens another."
- Proverbs 27:17

Have you thought about how the people in your life are affecting you? Are your friends and family pushing you to become a better person or letting you settle for a mediocre life? To have success and accomplish the dreams you have always wanted, it is important to surround yourself with people who will help you achieve those things. This does not always mean they will cheer you on; it might mean that they are going to make you into a tougher individual. If you are friends with the smartest people in your class and want to see them succeed, you will push them to always do better. Likewise, they will do the same for you. It might not always be fun because when you are holding each other accountable, there will be times when your friends will get on you for not doing the best you can do. The same can be said with your family if they are not seeing you succeed. Do not take these criticisms to heart. They are not against you; they are against you failing. In the end, you will be thankful for the levels they hold you to because it is only at these high levels can you obtain success.

January 22nd

"There is nothing permanent except change."
- Heraclitus: Ancient Greek Philosopher

You are beginning a new chapter in your life by going to college. This means that you will have another chapter to close. Your high school chapter has been completed, and you are starting something new. This can be sad because of all the fun memories and friends you made in high school. When you go off to college, you and your high school friends will be off on your separate ways, and you might fall out of contact with some of them. You are on your own for probably the first time in your life. It can be a bit scary when you are alone at this giant school surrounded by new people. You need to look at this as the beginning of a new chapter in your life. Sure, the last one was great, and you might be sad to see it go. This new chapter will be even better. You are going to meet so many new and interesting people, take interesting classes, and expand your intellect on different subjects. You will get to experience so many firsts in this new chapter of college. Do not be upset over the closing of your last chapter, but be excited for the beginning of this new one.

January 23rd

"I would rather die of passion than of boredom."

- Vincent Van Gogh: 19th Century Dutch Painter

What criteria went into choosing your major? Usually, you look to see if it has a good job outlook or will get you into grad school. Hopefully, one of the top reasons you chose the major you did was a passion for it. You will see people choose their majors and even their jobs because they make good money. Still, they are absolutely miserable at school or in their career. Sure, money is nice, but is it worth taking all the joy out of your work? Money is not going to buy you satisfaction in a job; only a love for the work will. Think about how much of your life you will spend working. Why would you want to work that long in an industry or field that you dislike? If you are not passionate about the field, you should look for some other area that you may be more interested in. You are going to graduate one day and begin your job. You do not want to be miserable working at it. This makes your life bad and everyone else's life bad around you. Find the field you are passionate about, and like they say, you will never work a day in your life.

January 24th

"The happiness of your life depends upon the quality of your thoughts."

- Marcus Aurelius: Roman Emperor & Stoic Philosopher

College is stressful for everyone. Life in general is often stressful for everyone. There will be times when the quality of your thoughts is pretty negative. You may spend several nights lying awake thinking about not being good enough for someone. Maybe you do not feel like you did as well on a test as you would have wanted, or the pressures of college are weighing on you. We have all had days where all you can think about is negativity. It is hard to believe that the thoughts inside our heads can completely affect things outside of us. If life is bad on the outside because of your beliefs, it is possible to change that. As simple as it sounds, you just need to think more positively. The happier you think, the happier you live. It is easier said than done, and it is hard starting off. Start small and begin each day by thinking of a couple of things that you appreciate. Once you have those good thoughts, you just have to consciously stop yourself when those bad ones start to creep in. Once you begin to do this, you will see the quality of your life inside and out improve.

January 25th

"Patience is the best remedy for every trouble."
- *Titus Maccius Plautus: Roman Playwright*

In no other period in history could you get what you needed as quickly as you can today. Think about how quickly you can get information or how fast you can have something delivered to you. The speed at which we have to get things is amazing, but it does have some downsides. One of the biggest ones is that we lose patience much quicker because everything is so fast. Patience is a key virtue that everyone should learn, including myself. Sometimes, you just have to wait. If you are studying for a test, you will not always retain all the information you have learned the first time. It usually requires that you practice it a few times to really understand it. Some people will study a subject, and if they do not get it the first time they study, they give up. Sometimes you have to wait a little longer to get something than what you want. It is not necessarily bad that you have to wait longer; if anything, it really helps you understand and practice patience. Not everything will unfold quickly. Have a bit of patience, and everything will work out in the end.

January 26th

"I pay no attention whatever to anybody's praise or blame. I simply follow my own feelings."

- Wolfgang Amadeus Mozart: 18th Austrian Century Composer

When you have a dream, you are always striving to obtain it. Suppose it is a dream of yours and other people know about. In that case, you are likely to draw some criticism for it. People will criticize you for anything. If you are opening a new business, they will say that you are too young or inexperienced. If you make it to a prestigious college, people will say that you did not work hard enough and got in by luck. They will talk about you as an athlete, student, or self-employee. There is no reason to listen to these people. Usually, people do not want to see you succeed because your success makes them look bad in comparison. If you have goals of success, then there will always be people criticizing you because they never had that success. Ignore their critiques of what you are doing. You have bigger and better goals that you are chasing rather than worrying about what people have to say about your goals in life.

January 27th

"Your own soul is nourished when you are kind; it is destroyed when you are cruel."

- King Solomon: Biblical King

There is no downside to being kind to others. We are not always kind to one another when we should be. No one should preach to you about something they are not perfect at. So, we should figure out a way to start being kinder to others. We often get caught up in the moment, and we let our emotions get the better of us. This usually means that we say or do something that we would not have done in a better mindset. When we act like this, it shows others that we are cruel, even if that is not the type of person we want to be. It is probably best to think about what you will say or do before acting on it. Thinking requires that your mind not be clouded by emotions. Getting rid of the emotional fog allows you to make a rational choice. We are rationally good; we just do not always portray our thoughts and actions rationally. Try to be more kind to others, because not only will it make their day better, but yours as well.

January 28th

"To face challenges with a calm mind robs misfortune of its' strength and burden."

- Lucius Annaeus Seneca: Roman Stoic Philosopher

Life is guaranteed to have challenges in them. When you are in college, this is your first time when you might have to face a majority of these challenges alone. No one can really prepare you for them; it is just something you figure out as you go. A big thing that will help you is keeping your cool when faced with a challenge. Probably the worst thing to do when facing adversity is to react. Getting angry, mad, upset, or even scared will make it that much harder to figure out a solution. All these emotions cloud your judgment and generally make it hard to think straight. Give yourself a second to catch your breath and keep your cool. Being calm in the face of adversity allows you to think clearly enough to make the best possible decision. Being relaxed in these situations is not something everyone is born with and will require some practice. There will be times when your emotions get the better of you, but if you can limit those times, you will make better decisions with better outcomes for yourself.

January 29th

"He is happy whom circumstances suit his temper; but he is more excellent who suits his temper to any circumstance."

- David Hume: 18th Century Scottish Philosopher

It is pretty easy to be happy and have a good temper when everything is going your way. There are just times in life when it feels like nothing in your life could go wrong. While this is nice, it is worth noting that not every day will be like this for you. How are you going to act when things do not go your way? You will see people around your age lose it when things are not going their way in life. They might have failed a test and got into an argument with their significant other. Sure, none of that is fun, but that should not give you a free pass to borderline throw a tantrum. People will tell you that they are mature, but wait and see how they act when life gives them some tough moments before you accept their claim. A real sign of maturity is not letting any situation phase you too badly. People who are only happy when everything around them benefits them are not really that grown-up yet. It is always more admirable if you can keep your cool in any situation, good or bad.

January 30th

"Those who guard their mouths and their tongues keep themselves from calamity."

- Proverbs 21: 23

It can get old listening to people tell you to "watch what you say," and you probably never thought much of this saying. You probably figured it was because people older than you did not like something you said. However, there is truth behind that quote. It is amazing how the less you say, the less trouble you make for yourself. Many people think they can talk themselves out of a situation. Well, for every person who talked themselves out of a problem, there have been ten who just made it worse. Communicating with others is a critical skill that everyone should learn. Learning to keep your mouth shut is an equally important skill that everyone should know. More often than not, when watching people try to talk themselves out of something, it just does not end well. If you really want to keep yourself out of bad situations, it is recommended that you just do not talk. Try it, and you will see just how amazing it can be.

January 31st

"I do what is mine to do; the rest does not disturb me."

- Marcus Aurelius: Roman Emperor & Stoic Philosophe

♦

Whether you are at work, at college, or even both, there are times when you feel like you have too much to do and not enough time to do it. This is a great opportunity to take a step back and figure out what is yours to do, and what is not your problem. Those homework assignments that need to get done, yup, those are yours to do. An exam that is later this week that you have not studied for, that is also yours to do. Take the time to figure out a plan to knock out those assignments and study up for that test. Do not let outside distractions block you from this. Do not let those notifications on your phone distract you from finishing that paper. Those notifications will still be there once you are finished. Whatever friends want to hang out can wait another hour for you to get your stuff finished. If you do not let those distractions get in the way, you will have less to worry about and more concentration on the task at hand. This makes it infinitely easier to get stuff done and do it with less worry and stress.

February

February 1st

"A danger foreseen is half avoided."
- English Proverb

A problem that many college students face is spreading their time and energy out among too many activities. Many students are taking upwards of fifteen credit hours as well as working a job to pay for tuition on top of trying to keep a social life. When you try to juggle too many tasks at once, they will all fail. What you do not want to happen is you become so overwhelmed that your grades, work, and social life begin to suffer. To counter this issue, you should plan out what you find most valuable to you and stick to that. If paying for college is a serious struggle for you, then you might want to focus more on working enough to cover tuition. In order to do this, you might have to take fewer credit hours in college. Because you are thinking about these possible problems now, you can avoid them in the future. Too often, college students get so committed to their obligations that when they become overwhelmed, they have no way out. If you take the time to plan for possible issues that may arise in your future, then you can avoid those issues.

February 2nd

"Dare to know! Have the courage to use your own intelligence."

- Immanuel Kant: 18th Century German Philosopher

The purpose of college is to better understand the world and the particular subjects that you are interested in. Sometimes, people will go to college just to say that they went, with no real passion or purpose behind their decision. If you want to go to college, you should desire to study and learn more about something. If you are interested in mathematics, use that interest to understand and learn as much as possible about that subject. You can also have multiple interests. That is the great thing about college: You can study so many different subjects that you are interested in. Another great thing is that you do not have to stick with one subject your whole college career. If you have a change of interest, you can absolutely switch. If you are no longer interested in mathematics but now have a strong interest in history, go learn as much as you can about history. Why not learn about everything that you can? You are an intelligent person, and you can always learn more. Use these capabilities to learn as much as you can. Whatever it is that interests you, learn about it.

February 3rd

"A man who cannot tolerate small misfortunes can never accomplish great things."

- Chinese Proverb

Nothing in life is going to go completely smoothly. There will be little nuisances that are always present in what you are doing. You will have people get under your skin and have situations pop up that really annoy you. These distractions will always happen, and you have to be able to power through them and not let them get you down. It can be easy to get down on yourself based on what someone said about you or how a certain situation played out. You may have gotten a low grade on your last test, and that can be pretty disappointing. You have to think about your ultimate goal of that class, which is to pass. Even if you want to pass with a good grade, the worst thing you can do is let one grade get you down. These are pretty small problems in your life in the grand scheme of things. Just remember that these issues are minuscule and do not matter. You are going to accomplish big things in your life, so do not let the little problems of life set you off course.

February 4th

"If people know how hard I had to work to gain my mastery, it would not seem so wonderful at all."

- Michelangelo: 16th Century Italian Sculptor & Painter

You are going to start learning in college that there are a lot of students and not that many teachers. Suppose you want to accomplish anything through college. In that case, you will probably have to beat out many people, between scholarships, academic awards, athletic awards, and even sometimes just clubs. These are all things where you will have to prove that you are better than everyone else to get in. So, if you really want these things, then prove to everyone that you are that person. You will have to outwork a lot of people, but if you are really determined, this will not be so hard. If it is academic awards, start outperforming everyone in the classroom. If you are a student athlete after some athletic awards, you will have to start out working with everyone on the field. It will be hard; you are probably working against a bunch of people with the same goal as you. So go out and work as hard as you can toward that goal, to the point that no one can ignore your skills.

February 5th

"A 'no' uttered from deepest conviction is better than a 'yes' merely uttered to please, or worse, to avoid trouble."

- Mahatma Gandhi: 20th Century Indian Lawyer & Political Ethicist

---

College is a time when you are finally your own person. You are free to make your own choices and do the things you want and do not want to do. You will make tons of friends, and their choices will not always align with yours. You must learn to set some self-boundaries for yourself. If you do not want to do something, you have the free choice to say no. You might be a people pleaser and never want to make anyone upset with you. While it is good to want to make others happy, you should never have to make others happy at the cost of your own happiness. You have your own goals in life, and those do not always align with others. If your goal is to make straight A's this semester, you may have to say no to a few parties. You should never feel bad about saying no because it is your choice, and you have the right to that choice. Do not feel like you have to say yes to everything just so you won't make others feel bad. Make the choice that feels best to you.

February 6th

"Chance is always powerful. Let your hook always be cast; in the pool where you least expect it, there will be fish."

- Ovid: Ancient Roman Poet

Probably one of the worst things you can say in life is "What if?" It will always be a question no matter how you arrange it. It is bad because you will live your entire life not knowing about that thing until you try it. How do you know you do not like that subject until you take that class? How do you know you do not like that person until you talk to them? This question is the biggest eliminator of opportunity. Once you try it, you will be able to say you do not like it, or you try it and you realize that you love it. Someday you will be too old to try the things you can try now. Depending on what you do now, you will look back and be satisfied with all that you tried and learned. None of us like the feeling of regret. Think about how those feelings feel now, and imagine what it would feel like if you let it set for fifty years. Live your life to the fullest, and try things even if you are not sure you will like them. At least when you look back, you can say, "I did."

February 7th

"Fall seven times, stand up eight."
- *Japanese Proverb*

◆

You are going to fall several times throughout college. Not literally (though you might fall physically some too), but in terms of failing. There will be times when college or even life knocks you down. You are going to fail at something in a class. You might fail an assignment, a paper, or even a test. What matters is not that you failed but that you got back up and kept going. You will have your heart broken, and it will suck, but as long as you do not give up and keep going, that is what matters. It is not wrong to fall; it is only bad when you fall and stay down. There is more to life than one failed test or relationship. You are bound to pass many more tests and fall in love with many more people. The only way you can do this, though, is if you keep going. So, do not give up and stay down because the only way to move on is to get back up. You feel miserable now after the post-failed test or post-breakup. If you decide that you will not let that define you and keep going, that is what true strength is—getting up after being knocked down.

February 8th

"You have power over your mind- not outside events. Realize this, and you will find strength."

- Marcus Aurelius: Roman Emperor & Stoic Philosopher

Wouldn't it be cool to control different external things with your mind? That might be one of the coolest superpowers to have. Unfortunately, we do not have the power to control external things with our minds. What we can control, though, is the mind itself. We have no control when all of your professors assign a paper and test the same week for all of your classes. This is something that is completely out of our control. We can control how we think and how we react to this. Sure, this is not ideal for you, but there is not a lot you can do about it. We will have to accept that this might suck a little bit and roll with the punches. We can also tell ourselves that we will survive, and we will come out on top of this unscathed. If you keep control of yourself and do not act irrationally, you truly do have full control of yourself. And when you have full control of yourself, you can tackle any challenge you have to face.

February 9th

"Do little things now; so shall big things come to thee by and by asking to be done."

- Persian Proverb

We often have a misconception of what greatness looks like. If you want to do something great, it usually means doing something big. As a college student, you probably have very little access to do something huge. You are not old enough or do not have the financial means to change the world. This is not meant to discourage you from trying to do something big. It means that instead of looking at what big thing you can do, rather look at the small steps you can take to complete this big thing. Sometimes to do something great, you have to do many little things really well. You are going to do a bunch of things that feel pretty insignificant. Still, when you look back, you will realize that they were the foundation that allowed you to climb to the top for your big goal. Do not be discouraged if you start off by doing small tasks. Whether you think it or not, it is making a difference. You will get to complete big things one day; it just might mean starting with something a bit smaller.

February 10th

"Let silence be your general rule; say only what is necessary and in few words."

- Epictetus: Ancient Greek Philosopher

Something that you may start to notice is that people talk way too much. This is just a general observation, and not one directly pointed at anyone. People often talk more than is necessary, which tends to put them in bad positions. Sometimes sitting back and just listening can be beneficial for you and everyone around. You will have professors and students get agitated when students in class talk nonstop. They will give presentations and drag it on just talking about random topics. Usually, there is nothing wrong with keeping talks short and sweet. There are times when long and drawn-out conversations are absolutely okay. Still, generally, it is best to stick to short and sweet. Sitting and listening are skills that will serve everyone well. People will be more likely to talk to you if you sit there and listen. You will generally benefit from listening and not speaking most of the time. What gets people in trouble is that they do not know when to stop and end up saying something they could have avoided if they would have stopped. Say what you need to say, and that usually gets the job done.

February 11th

"Everything we hear is an opinion, not a fact. Everything we see is a perspective, not the truth."

- Marcus Aurelius: Roman Emperor & Stoic Philosopher

We have all heard it before: "What you see on social media is not the whole truth." This saying is a broken record that you have listened to more than enough times. You cannot base your thoughts on what you see on the internet. You can also not base your life on what you see others do on social media. You only see the best of others on social media. Very rarely do you ever see the bad of someone else's life being posted on Instagram. Most of what you read on social media is not always 100 percent truthful. You might see someone in what looks like the happiest relationship ever on Instagram, but that is the perspective they want everyone to see. What you might not see is a loveless relationship. The statistic you see on Twitter might have been intentionally manipulated to show the statistics it wants, rather than what is truthful. Take everything you read on social media with a grain of salt because it usually is not all that great. People often change the truth to better benefit themselves, remember that.

February 12th

"Success usually comes to those who are too busy to be looking for it."

- Henry David Thoreau: 19th Century American Writer & Philosopher

---

You might be wondering how to start having success in something. You can go read websites and books about what to do to have the best chances of having success. Actually, you just need to begin. If you start working at it, you will continue to improve. You will have failure, which will lead to more knowledge and experience in what you are working on. You are busy learning and perfecting your craft. This is when success happens. You are not trying to find success. It found you. You were not perfecting whatever you were doing for success. You are practicing it to get better, so eventually, success will happen. If you are hoping to just wait for success to accidentally happen to you, then you are probably not ever going to obtain it. So go out and get busy doing whatever you want to have success in because the more active you are perfecting it, the more likely success will come. You will be so busy perfecting that you are going to forget why you started, and when success shows up, you will have a nice surprise in store for you.

February 13th

"Yesterday I was clever, so I wanted to change the world. Today I am wise, so I am changing myself."

- Rumi: 13th Century Persian Poet

It is easy to think about how you can change the world. Maybe you want to be a doctor and save lives, or you want to go into foreign diplomacy and end tensions with other countries. As you get older, you begin to realize just how hard these things are. Not only do they require a lot of effort on your part, but they also require equal effort from other people. You might start to think that you really cannot change anything. While those options are still possible, there is one thing you can always change much easier: yourself. You are in complete control of what you want to do and have the option to change yourself in any way that you please. You can get into the best shape of your life. You can gain knowledge if you do not feel smart enough. It usually requires no one else's help, and you can always continue to improve yourself, so there is no limit to it. While it is possible to change the world, it is highly recommended that you also take the opportunity to work and change yourself for the better.

February 14th

"Don't listen to what they say. Go see."
- Chinese Proverb

It is not as easy to get out and see the world as some people say. Regardless of a global pandemic, some things will just get in the way, it could be a grueling school schedule, family responsibilities, or financial reasons. However, you do not have to go far to get out and experience the world. You can usually experience a lot by just going out close to where you live. Go out with friends and try some of the new restaurants and bars in your college town. You can usually find a pretty cool lake or wilderness area to just go relax. Believe it or not, your college campus probably has some pretty cool spots to go exploring too. It is not as much fun to just sit around and listen to what other people are doing and finding out; you should find out for yourself. A big part of growing up is learning to go out, even if it is by yourself, and just spending some time exploring the world around you. You might not get the massive cultural differences you would if you traveled abroad, but you get a little bit of something new and different to you. Just think, if worse comes to worst, at least you will find some good places to eat.

February 15th

"We suffer more often in imagination than in reality."
- Lucius Annaeus Seneca: Roman Stoic Philosopher

Is this test going to be the hardest test you have ever taken, or are you just overthinking it? Does this new girl or guy really like you, or are you overthinking your relationship? That little voice in your head can often be more negative than we want it to be. Much of what you are worrying about is a fear that your mind has created more than it is reality. You would be amazed how much better your life will be when you are able to shut out these negative thoughts and replace them with positive ones. An easy example is rather than thinking, There is no way I am going to pass this exam, you should think, I can totally pass this exam. This positive thinking may not mean that you will do good on the exam, but you will go into it with enough confidence that at least you can say that you gave it your best shot. By just thinking more positively, it can help you make it through some tough exams more than when you have negative thoughts. Life is too short to think negatively; it is time to replace those doubts with confident thoughts!

February 16th

"When walking, walk. When eating, eat."

- Zen Proverb

Some people think they have to reinvent everything about themselves to succeed. They really do not have to do as much as they believe. To have success, you need to have some serious focus on what you want to be successful at. Suppose you're going to be a successful college student. In that case, you will have to put almost all your focus on your classes, homework, exams, etc. Suppose you want to be a successful athlete. In that case, you will have to focus on school, workouts, workout recovery, and performing well in games. Focusing on your goals is what is going to get you the success you want. If you get distracted by every small thing, how will you make the appropriate decisions you need to? It is incredibly difficult to accomplish something if you keep getting distracted. If you focus on your goals, success will start to focus on you. Focus on one thing at a time, and it is easier to get everything accomplished. You do not need to be a whole new person to do this. You just need to focus on what you want.

February 17th

"Twenty years from now you will be more disappointed by the things that you didn't do than by the ones you did do."

- Mark Twain: 19th Century American Writer

It is always rather sad when listening to adults talk about what they regretted not doing when they were younger. It is sad because you cannot help but think of how much different their lives would be if they would not have given up on a dream or made some other decisions along the road. It is easy to brush these off as adults just reminiscing about their past. However, you should take these as a warning. Someday you will be those adults. Are you going to be talking about all the things you wished you did differently or about how grateful you are that you made the right decisions? College is a great time to experiment with what you will and will not enjoy. How do you know if you will like something if you do not try it? If the absolute worst thing you say to yourself is, "Hey, I do not really like this," then that is a lot better than, "Man, I wish I would have at least tried that back in college." Not liking something will be better than regretting not trying it in the first place.

February 18th

"The person who has many faults is usually the first to criticize others."

- Korean Proverb

When you start to have success, critics soon show up. Unfortunately, people will put you down for the success that you have gained. If you do not know how to deal with people criticizing you, it can upset you. It is important to know that people who blame others are usually not happy with their own lives. They put others down because they cannot stand to see someone they know having more success than them. They have a lot of maturing that they need to work on if seeing someone else succeed makes them act like that. These people really have nothing better to do than put you down, which is pretty sad. Do not concern yourself with these people. You are so far ahead of them in life that it would be foolish to stop and look back and acknowledge what they have to say. You have dreams to chase and things to accomplish. You do not have time to listen to what people are saying behind your back. Keep having the success you deserve and not giving your critics any attention. That is something that they do not deserve.

February 19th

"You always have the option of having no opinion."
- Marcus Aurelius: Roman Emperor & Stoic Philosopher

You are going to learn a lot during college. A majority of it will be learning inside the classroom. However, another large amount will be stuff you learn outside the classroom. You will learn about other people and other subjects that do not really have to do with college classes. Many people will ask you what you think of this person or that person. They may also ask what you think of a specific predicament. All of these people want your opinion in some way or another. Many times, you are asked for an opinion on something, and you honestly have no idea about anything on the subject or person. It is never wrong to say that you have no opinion on the matter; sometimes it is best to just have no opinion. It may not be the answer people want to hear, but it will be the most truthful answer that you give. Do not provide untrue opinions. You do not have to know everything; it is okay to have no knowledge of a subject or person. Therefore, it is all right to just say, "Hey, I do not know much about it; I do not really have an opinion."

February 20th

"Man is a mystery. It needs to be unraveled, and if you spend your whole life unravelling it, don't say that you've wasted time. I am studying that mystery because I want to be a human being."

- Fyodor Dostoevsky: 19th Century Russian Novelist

While you go to college to learn about the major of your choice, you also have the opportunity to learn a lot about yourself. It is not often talked about, but learning about who you are is very important. It is not a difficult thing to accomplish. You just have to spend some time with yourself and just yourself. If you never figure out who you are, you really do not know your purpose. What is your aim in life? What about your dreams? Why should anyone get to know you if you do not know yourself? The person that you spend the most time with is you. Take the time to get to know yourself and find out the real you. The person you think you are might have changed since the last time you thought about it. You are changing all the time, so you have to make sure that you keep up. You can always change your major and change your classes, but you are stuck with yourself; you might as well get to know yourself.

February 21st

"Go confidently in the direction of your dreams! Live the life you've imagined."

- Henry David Thoreau: 19th Century American Writer & Philosopher

---

You are probably now imagining what you want to do in life. We all have dreams that we are out to obtain. College is kind of the first time in your life when you have the most freedom to go out and see those dreams of yours. You might be scared or nervous about chasing your dreams. If you really care about obtaining them, you will throw fear out the window and start chasing. Go work toward your goals and do what you must to get to them. Some people do not always want to see you complete your dreams, which is okay. Not everyone is meant to stay in your life forever, and if they are not going to help support you toward your dreams, then it might be best to let them go. You will have to make some sacrifices on your way to completing your goals. While that seems daunting, it will be all worth it once you have achieved your goals. So go out and chase those crazy goals and dreams of yours. Do not worry about what others think of you. In the end, as long as you are satisfied with the plans you completed, that is all that matters.

February 22nd

"New beginnings are often disguised as painful endings."
- Lao Tzu: Ancient Chinese Philosopher

There will be things that suck about your life. You will fail a test in your class, you have a falling out with a friend, or your girlfriend or boyfriend will leave you. What really sucks is when several of these happen in the same week. You cannot control that your significant other was flirting with other people for months before they left you. Or that they lost feelings and led you on for a month. You can be angry and sad and frustrated, but nothing will change what they did to you. You just have to keep living, day by day, and do whatever you can to move on. You no longer talking to your longtime friend sucks, but it happens. Not everyone is meant to be in our lives forever. When you lose one friend, you are bound to pick up another. There are times when everything is stacked against you to pass this test. You do not understand the material, and you stayed up all night studying. You get to the exam confused and tired. In all these situations, the only thing you can do is to keep plugging along. You are stuck in a rut right now, but as long as you keep moving, you will not be there forever.

February 23rd

"Start by doing what's necessary; then do what's possible; and suddenly you are doing the impossible."

- St. Francis of Assisi: 12th Century Italian Catholic Frier

You are looking at the syllabus for your new class, and wow, did you pick a tough course! You are looking at the number of assignments and tests and how much they are all worth. Unfortunately for you, you have to take this class for your major. You are now asking yourself how you will make it through this semester and questioning if passing this class is even possible. Well, you could drop this class and change your major, or you could tell yourself that this class is not impossible, and you are going to give it your best shot. The only way this class will be impossible is if you do not take it. Once you start your journey in this class, you will soon find your rhythm and get the hang of it. You quickly realize that this class is not impossible. Rather, your judgment on the course a few weeks ago was very flawed. Do not run away from those impossible classes. Do not run away from those impossible issues. They will quickly become possible if you take some time to work on them.

February 24th

"Associate with people who are likely to improve you."

- Lucius Annaeus Seneca: Roman Stoic Philosopher

If you did not have a great group of friends in high school, college is a great time to find new ones. There are big groups and organizations where you can find people with common interests. If you had a group of friends who were constantly bringing you down and never helped or pushed you to reach your goals, then they really are not the best friends for you. Find a new group of friends who want the very best for you. When you stop and consider which friends are not pushing you for the best, you might be surprised by how many true friends you are left with. These other friends might be someone you enjoy hanging out with but do not have your best interest at heart. Your real friends will not let you settle for anything less than your desired goals. Why would you want to surround yourself with people who do not want the best for you? You have to choose between these two groups. The group of people who hold you back versus those who push you. You might not always like having people encourage you for greatness, but in the end, you will be glad that they did.

February 25th

"No man ever steps in the same river twice, for it's not the same river and he's not the same man."

- Heraclitus: Ancient Greek Philosopher

It can be very intimidating to go back to a situation that you have failed previously. In college, you can feel a lot of pressure taking your second exam if you have failed the first. It is important to remember that you are not who you were the last time you took that test. It does not matter if that test was yesterday or a month ago; you are a different person. You might be wondering, How am I any different than before? The simple answer is that you are older and wiser. Even if you are a day older, you have experienced failure with that last test, and it is a feeling you do not want to feel anymore. You now know what you did wrong and are changing that to ensure that failure does not happen again. You know more than you did last time. It is nice to know that you can always change. If you fail at something once, you will be a different person the next time you try. Everything is always changing, including you, so do not worry if you fail once; try again. You are a completely different person this time around.

February 26th

"Life can only be understood backwards; but it must be lived forwards."

- Soren Kierkegaard: 18th century Danish Philosopher

When we think about our lives, we can only recollect on the past and what has already happened. We really have no way of understanding anything in the future because it has not happened yet. The only way you can appreciate the life that you have lived is to look back on it. Sure, it can be fun to reminisce on the past and think of all the good times that you had. It is even good to think back on the mistakes you have made so you can learn from them and apply that new knowledge in the future. You will never know what it is like to live unless you look forward rather than back. You cannot live in the past; it will only end up hurting you more. It can be easy to stay in the past because we are comfortable there. Staying in one familiar place forever is not how a person was meant to live. You will have to take that leap of faith into the unknown of the future. Yes, it is scarier than where you have been. Still, it is also more exciting and leads to so many different opportunities. You only live one way, and that is forward. So, focus your attention forward rather than backward.

February 27th

"Courage is the first of human qualities because it is the quality which guarantees the others."

- Aristotle: Ancient Greek Philosopher

Getting out of your comfort zone will be a big learning curve when you go to college. No matter what type of personality you are, you will be put in situations where you feel you have little knowledge and are uncomfortable. Suppose you want to have success in a college class. In that case, you will probably have to push yourself academically harder than you did in high school. Another big thing you will have to learn is asking for help. You are not going to know how to do everything, and that is okay, but it will require getting some assistance. It might be from a professor or from a friend. This can be big for someone who hated asking people for help. This will require you to get out of your comfort zone, open up, and ask for some help. If you never ask for help, no one will ever think to help you. If you want to be a successful person, get out of your comfort zone to grow as a person. If you're going to see change and growth, you will have to leave your comfort zone.

February 28th

"Tranquility within consists in the good ordering of the mind."

- Marcus Aurelius: Roman Emperor & Stoic Philosopher

One of the most unpleasant feelings is lying in bed and you cannot go to sleep because your mind is racing with about a million different thoughts. Most of the time, these are not the best quality thoughts either. College and early adulthood lead to many times of uncertainty. This uncertainty can be anything from wondering if you are good enough for someone else, smart enough to even go to college, or how you will be able to afford all the college expenses. There are hundreds of different negative thoughts that can creep into your head. You cannot live a good life with these thoughts buzzing around in your head. You need to fix it. You need to kick those bad thoughts out and unscramble the rest. Sometimes you just have to tell yourself that you are good enough and can do it. Giving yourself mental pep talks really seems to help. Anxious thoughts about future events can be written on paper. This can help get these thoughts out of your head so you can relax. The only thing you have room for now is good thoughts. Once you have allowed yourself room for only those, you will find peace.

February 29th

"Be yourself; everyone else is already taken."
- *Oscar Wilde: 19th Century Irish Poet*

Your time in college is limited. It would not be the wisest thing to stay in college for the rest of your life. This is one of the most fun times in your life, so do not waste it because you do things you do not want to do. Would it not stink to look back at college in thirty years and think about all the things you wish you had done differently? When you first get to college, you will meet so many different people, and they are all going to want to do some other things. If your friends are staying in and you want to go to a party, then go to the party. Sure, there are times when you need to compromise. You cannot make everything about you all the time. You also do not want to just give up on what you want to do because you do not want to be the odd person out. Do not just tag along with everyone because you are afraid of being different. Go out and do what you want because this is your only time in college. You are your own unique individual. You might as well live it the way you want. You do not want to change who you are just to be like others.

March

March 1st

"What would life be if we had no courage to attempt anything?"

- *Vincent Van Gogh: 19th Century Dutch Painter*

What worked in high school will probably not work in college. No longer can you never study and get away with it. Something that you have to learn in college is how to study. Many college students never actually learned how to study, which is not good when you are in college. So, what did I do to find the best way to retain information? Trial and error. You try something, and if you fail, you do not do it anymore. Do that until you start to find ways to succeed. You can apply this to anything. Have trouble making friends? Start trying some new ways to interact with people. If they do not work, then do not use them. Go down the list of ways, and once you find the way that works, use that. There are just going to be times when you have to use some trial and error to figure out how to do something. Are you going to fail a few times? Yes. Will you eventually find a way to succeed, and everything will work out fine? Also, yes. Try it out, see if it works, and go from there. It kind of works for every situation you will encounter. If you had no courage to try and fail, then you would have never found the right answer.

March 2nd

"There are times where fear is good. It must keep its watchful place at the heart's control."

- Aeschylus: Ancient Greek Tragedian

Whether you are from a small-town high school or big-city high school, you might feel a bit overwhelmed with how big college can be. You might have become used to being the big fish in a small pond, and now you are a tiny fish in a big pond. This is probably the first time you are truly alone with no one looking out for you. You might be dealing with some new problems like high expectations of doing well in college or coping with being alone for the first time. You might also be dealing with relationship issues for the first time. Whatever it is that you are going through, you should not look at the fear that comes with these issues as bad, but rather as a chance to grow. The fear you feel is only because you have never gone through this situation before, so you fear the unknown. These issues allow you the opportunity to overcome these new fears and to learn about yourself. Fear is bound to show up when in college; use it as an opportunity for growth, rather than letting it prohibit you.

March 3rd

"Either do not begin or, having begun, do not give up."

- Chinese Proverb

The road to success is a long and rough one. It is not always easy to keep going, especially when you do not see any success. This is okay. This does not mean that you are doing it wrong; it just means that it will take some time before you start to see the rewards for your work. You are bound to encounter some issues along the way. You are going to have failures; you are going to have setbacks. These are just going to happen, but you cannot let these discourage you from continuing. Success is not something that everyone has. Most people encounter some hardships and then they give up. There will be times when you feel like giving up, but these failures happen right when you are about to see some successes. So, do not give up just because it is hard. Keep going because it means you are about due some of the achievements for your perseverance. You will get to the finish line eventually if you keep pushing along. If you give up, then you have no chance of getting to your goals. It might take some time, but as long as you keep going, you will get there.

March 4th

"We are what we repeatedly do. Excellence, therefore, is not an act, but a habit."

- Aristotle: Ancient Greek Philosopher

Habits are something that you will come to live by once you get settled in at college. Whether it be when you leave for class or decide to take a break during your day, you will repeatedly do the same thing every single day. These habits you build are just how you best perform during the day. Habits can either be good or bad. Unfortunately, if you make it a habit of skipping class and never doing your homework, you will not be in college for very long. These habits can be very easy to form. Maybe you decide to skip class and just relax at home one day. It is a lot easier to do that again the next day. Too many people fall into these bad habits. Luckily, if we decide to make a habit of good things, then it becomes a lot easier to do them. If you want to be great at something, you have to create habits that will positively affect you to move toward that greatness. You will not become an excellent student unless you make habits of being an outstanding student. If you do something enough times, it becomes a habit. Make sure that the habits you are making are ones that will positively affect you.

March 5th

"It is my bad luck that this has happened to me. No, you should rather say: It is my good luck that, although this has happened to me, I can bear it... so why see more misfortune in the event than good fortune in your ability to bear it?"

- Marcus Aurelius: Roman Emperor & Stoic Philosopher

◆

Does it seem like your professors got together and talked about when they could schedule their exams for the same week? Yup, been there before. You might be asking yourself, "Why is this happening to me this week?" Instead of making it negative, it might be better to spin it positively. For one, after this week is over, you will have all of your exams taken! A little deeper thought could be that this week is a chance to prove how determined and disciplined a student you are. While this week might suck, you are strong enough to bear this weight and prove to yourself and everyone else that you are pretty good at this whole college thing. Negative thinking will produce negative results. Going into the test week with negative thoughts bouncing around in your head will probably decrease those test scores. Go into this week believing that you can do it, and you are going to do it.

March 6th

"Don't grieve. Anything you lose comes around in another form."

- Rumi: 13th Century Persian Poet

There will be times in life when you lose. You might lose a friendship or lose a romantic relationship. It can be pretty tough to go through these events, and it is also pretty rough on your moral. You have lost a person who was a major part of your life. It is not easy to just move on when that constant presence is no longer there. Just because you lost someone does not mean that you are going to be without someone again. You will find a new friend, and you will find a new romantic relationship. It hurts now because you are going through the withdrawals of having that person, but pretty soon you will get over it. Typically, when you lose something, you gain something after. Sure, you might have had a rough breakup, but this could lead you to finding the love of your life. Your friendship with someone else is gone, but it now leaves an opportunity to have someone else become that new best friend. It is always hard to see the bright side of these situations when you are going through them, but you will be surprised at the good that comes out afterward.

March 7th

"To have courage for whatever comes in life – everything lies in that."

- *Saint Teresa of Avila: 16th Century Spanish Noblewoman*

◆

Whether you just succeeded or just failed, the sun will come up tomorrow, and it will be a new day. When you fall, it might feel like the world is coming to an end. Luckily for you, it is not. You will figure out how to fix this failure, and you will go on to have success. When you succeed at something, you feel awesome. You had a dream, then turned it into a goal, and then completed that goal. Well, now what? You achieved your goal, and now it should be on to the next one. Never be satisfied with where you are. Always keep aiming higher and higher. Both success and failure require that you dare to keep going. In defeat, you must have the courage to return from a setback and continue forward. In victory, you must have the courage to set the bar higher and aim for a new goal. You do not know what is going to happen in the future, but you can face whatever it is with courage. If you keep your courage to continue on in failure and success, you will be unstoppable.

March 8th

"Even though you know a thousand things, ask the man who knows one."

- Turkish Proverb

You are in college, so you will learn so much about so many different topics. You might begin to think that you are pretty smart. While you might be pretty smart, do not think you are smart enough to pass up some more information. You can learn a lot from people you might not perceive to be as smart as you. Everyone has their own life with their own unique experiences. This means that they probably know something that you do not. Talk to these people and learn as much as you can from every person you meet. It might just result in you having a nice conversation with someone. Better yet, that nice conversation could instill some wisdom upon you that will help you not make the same mistakes or make the same good choices that they did. It is wrong to write someone off because you think you have more knowledge than them. While you might have more knowledge in some areas, they might be smarter than you in others. So, use that as an opportunity to widen your areas of expertise and learn something you did not know.

March 9th

"Loss is nothing else but change, and change is nature's delight."

- Marcus Aurelius: Roman Emperor & Stoic Philosopher

Change is something that will be inevitable during college. You will change friends, significant others, classes, and maybe even majors. Do not be upset when change happens; instead, welcome it with open arms. Not everything is supposed to stay in your life forever. Change is how we learn to grow and mature. At first, change can be difficult. It is easy to get used to having everything in your life be the same forever. You should be open to new plans and people. It hurts when you date someone for so many years, only for them to leave out of nowhere. While it is natural to grieve a loss like this, you should also welcome the new opportunities that are open to you. You are single and free and have no one to answer to. This has just opened up countless opportunities for you to experience. At first, change can be sad and scary, but in time, you will realize how nice it can be. Always be open to what life brings to you. Instead of worrying about the unknown, welcome the unknown as something new and special for you to experience.

March 10th

"Patience and perseverance have a magical effect before which difficulties disappear and obstacles vanish."

- John Quincy Adams: 6th President of the United States

College is hard work. It is not all parties and good times like you might have thought. There is a certain amount of hard work you will have to do to succeed. Some of this hard work will require perseverance. You will have times when you have done hours of note-taking, and now you have to write a paper over those notes. You are mentally burnt out and do not feel like you can write. Sometimes you have to persevere through these hard times so you can get to the good. People will tell you that hard work will be met with a good reward at the end. Sometimes, your reward is just more work. You might have to do a few hard jobs before you get to the good. Being able to persevere through these times will get you the success and good that you want. If you can strive through the mental strain of writing this paper, you will be able to turn it in and be done with it. Persevering is not always fun, but it will help you tremendously in your college life.

March 11th

"The man who moves a mountain begins by carrying away small stones."

- Confucius: Ancient Chinese Philosopher

It can be easy to start daydreaming about all the goals you want to accomplish. You can think and dream about all the things you are going to do, but if you never go out and start working for them, they will continue to just be thoughts. Success comes when you start actually chasing after your dreams rather than just dreaming about them. If it helps, write down the goals, and put that list somewhere where you can see it every day. That way, instead of dreaming, you can look at it and decide how to plan your day to work toward your dreams. Go out and start working toward your goals. Sure, it is not always fun at the beginning when the success is not showing up. However, success will start to show up if you keep with it and continue to work at it every day. You will be glad that you started working toward your dreams rather than keeping them in your head. Your dreams might take some time, but that is only because they are big. Doing the small work every single day will lead you to obtaining your goals.

March 12th

"No one saves us but ourselves. No one can and no one may, we ourselves must walk the path."

- Buddha: Ancient Indian Religious Leader

If you go to just one class in college, you will realize that there are many people from a bunch of different backgrounds. There are first-generation students, and there are those whose family has been to college for many generations. Some students are eighteen-year-old freshmen, and you will have students in their late sixties going to school for fun. Where you came from before college does not matter; what matters is where you are going. To whom you are born, the parents that you have, and the neighborhood you grow up in is out of your control. Some people have a harder upbringing than others. College is a great chance to take control of your life and change it. You can create a better life for yourself and the people around you. Go out and make something of your life. Become a good student, get your college degree, and provide for yourself and those depending on you. While your background may have prevented you from doing something before, you now have the new opportunities in front of you to go somewhere better.

March 13th

"When everything seems to be going against you, remember that the airplane takes off against the wind, not with it."

- Henry Ford: 20th Century American Industrialist

There will be times when it feels like everyone, and the world, is against you. Nothing is going right, and you feel alone. Your significant other has left after a fight. You are studying for some pretty difficult classes, and there is a global pandemic. This might sound like something you may have gone through. Yes, it sucks, but what are you going to do about it? Think about how impressive it is that an airplane can lift off into the sky while flying into a headwind. Hundreds of passengers and tons of materials just fly away; that's pretty impressive. Your resilience against everything happening in your life is also pretty remarkable. Just as a plane will land, so will the issues that are happening in your life. Soon, the problems in your relationship and your schoolwork will subside and get easier. Being able to power through the problems in your life will always lead to the pleasures on the other side.

March 14th

"A fool is known by his speech, and a wise man by silence."

- Pythagoras: Ancient Greek Philosopher

We all know that one person who talks way too much and always gets themselves in trouble. You have probably spoken with your friends about something stupid someone said. It is not always good to be known as the person who said something stupid. Most people who talk loudly and arrogantly only confirm what is known about them: a fool. However, I do not remember when saying nothing got me known for something stupid. Knowing when to speak and when to shut up is a tool that will help you out more than you know. Not only will it keep you out of trouble, but more people will listen to you. The more you sit and watch in silence, the more foolish you realize most people make of themselves. After a while, people realize that a fool talks just to be heard, while someone much wiser who talks less, knows that everything they have to say is worth listening to. You would be amazed how many more people will listen to you when you stop talking so much.

March 15th

"The soul becomes dyed with the color of its thoughts."

- Marcus Aurelius: Roman Emperor & Stoic Philosopher

College can be a time full of new people and new experiences. It can also be the first time that you are really alone. When you are alone, it is just you and your thoughts. If you have those good thoughts flowing, it is actually enjoyable to be by yourself. You really can enjoy yourself. If you can enjoy yourself, then most likely, that means that everyone else will appreciate you too. However, if you have bad thoughts flowing through you, you will struggle to be alone. Being able to take the necessary steps to get those bad thoughts out will be really important. There is no fix-all solution to this. Find things you really enjoy about yourself and focus on those. That way, when you have those bad thoughts, you can drown them out with positive ones. Once you can get those good thoughts going, you are more enjoyable with other people. However, you are also more enjoyable with yourself. Take the time to fill your mind with positive and constructive thoughts, and life will become more pleasurable.

March 16th

"The work praises the man."

- Irish Proverb

It is pretty easy to get used to people praising you for every good thing you do. This can actually lead to a pretty bad ending if you are not careful. If you only do something so you can get praised for it, and you end up not being honored, then you probably will stop doing that thing. For example, this can lead to a quick end to education because you will not be praised for everything you do right. You should learn to be honored by your work, rather than by other people admiring your work. At first, it does not feel rewarding. There are no words of affirmation or pats on the back. Eventually, you will start to get the feeling of accomplishment you got from others by just looking at your good work. When you look at the score you got on your last test, the score speaks for itself. You no longer need someone to cheer you on; you can do it yourself. It is much better to let your work do the praise for you rather than others. It is more low-key, and it feels more personal to you. Feel good about a job well done, even if no one is there to see it.

March 17th

"Whatever you are, be a good one."
- Abraham Lincoln: 16th President of the United States

◆

We are all in different situations when we are at college. Some people are trying to work to pay for school while also going to school. Others are not. Some are student athletes trying to balance a school schedule around practices and games. Some students are single, some are married, and some are even parents. We all have a different story we are trying to tell. Whatever you are trying to do, do it to the best of your abilities. If you are a student, be the best student you can possibly be. If you are an athlete, be the best athlete you can be. As you start to do this, you will notice that it will begin working into other parts of your life. You will start to become the best sibling, friend, and partner you can be. This will transfer into your future job. You will be the best doctor, nurse, lawyer, or engineer that you can be. If you are going to do something, do it to the best of your ability. There is no purpose to doing something with mediocrity. Think about your future job. Is anyone going to want an average doctor or lawyer? No, they want the best, so be the best.

March 18th

"Life grants nothing to us mortals without hard work."
- *Horace: Ancient Roman Lyric Poet*

You might think that success is a gift that is granted by fate. Maybe you believe that God's hand selected them for the success that they received. This may not be true. Usually, it is just a lot of hard work that people do not see. What is funny about success is that you will put in a lot of time, effort, and work while no one is looking, but once you start to reap the benefits of your work, people begin to notice. For example, if you want to succeed at this upcoming quiz, you will have to study all the material that might be on it. You will have to take notes then quiz yourself on the notes. Not many people will acknowledge all the work you are putting in for the quiz. However, when you ace the examination, everyone will start to notice. It is no secret why you succeeded; you put in the hard work, and it paid off. The harder the work you put in, the more likely you will have success. Do not think that people are simply gifted with success until you see the kind of work they put in when you are not looking. Go put in that hard work, and you will start to see success.

March 19th

"Disappointment is the nurse of wisdom."
- *Sir Boyle Roche: 18th Century Irish Politician*

Have you ever thought about all the what-ifs in your life? What if you had done this, or what if you had done that. When you think about these situations, it is not that you failed. It is actually that you did not try. Failing is not fun; usually, it is a huge blow to our confidence and self-esteem. A blown business idea or getting rejected when you ask someone out, ouch! You walk away from these situations disappointed and probably do not feel confident about yourself. You are not going to succeed at everything, and that is okay. What matters is that you tried. Failing is a part of life. You learn from your mistakes, and you use this newfound knowledge. You can apply it to similar situations in the future. You will learn new and better business ideas or not use those stupid pick-up lines again. When you look back, you will not regret these situations where you failed; rather, you will be glad that you at least tried. It is a lot better to look back and realize that you failed rather than ask yourself, "What if?"

March 20th

"My greatest concern is not whether you have failed, but whether you are content with your failure."

- Abraham Lincoln: 16th President of the United States

If you think about your class as a road, you have the starting point, which is the first class, and the finishing point, which is the last day of class. There are two different variations of the road: one to passing the class and one to failing the course. When you stand there at the starting line, these two variations will look almost identical. The reason for this is because, well, they are. The only difference is the finishing point, either success or failure. During your travel on this road throughout the semester, you will have failures and setbacks. You might think to yourself that because you have encountered these issues, it means you are on the path to failure. If you tell yourself that you failed and are just going to never get better at this subject, you might as well give up. However, suppose you can tell yourself that you will overcome these obstacles and continue persevering. In that case, you continue on the path of success. If you choose failure, you will end with that. Choose success, and you will finish with it.

March 21st

"If you are distressed by anything external, the pain is not due to the thing itself, but to your estimate of it; and this you have the power to revoke at any moment."

- Marcus Aurelius: Roman Emperor & Stoic Philosopher

◆

You will become very familiar with stress once you get into college. There will be many days of high-stress classes, work, money issues, etc. Have you ever wondered why certain things stress us out so much? Well, really, it is just because we think they are stressful. We have estimated something as being stressful, even if we have done that thing many times successfully. We have all taken exams in our lives, so why do we get so stressed going into a class to take a test? We want to do well, so we put pressure on ourselves to succeed. Have you ever tried thinking of this exam as super easy? It changes how stressed you are about it. We have the power to think of how stressful something is, yet we almost always allow stress to get the better of our thoughts. The less power you give to something, the less stress you will feel about that thing. Next time you feel stressed, just think about how you will overcome this obstacle and make it look easy. See, it kind of helps, doesn't it?

March 22nd

"It is in the character of very few men to honor without envy a friend who has prospered."

- Aeschylus: Ancient Greek Tragedian

You are going to do big things with your life. You are going to do big things in college. It is easy to feel good when everyone around you is not doing as well as you are. But when a close friend of yours starts to do things that propel them up, how are you going to feel about it? You will most likely be happy for them, but very few people actually put that to practice. Many of us are filled with envy and jealousy when someone close to us is doing well for themselves. Maybe this person beat you out for a scholarship or academic award. If your best friend did this, are you going to be able to feel happy for them, or are you going to be upset and filled with envy? Being able to graciously accept defeat without feeling jealousy for the other is a skill that is tough to acquire if you do not have it. You are not going to win everything. There will be times when you lose. If you can accept that you are human and not perfect, this is a step in the right direction. They are your friend for a reason. Treat them like one.

March 23rd

"Without continual growth and progress, such words as improvement, achievement, and success have no meaning."

- Benjamin Franklin: 18th Century Writer & Inventor

―――――――――――◆―――――――――――

One of the biggest mistakes you can make in college is thinking that the classes will get easier as you go along. You may think that as you progress through your courses that each semester should get easier for you. You are in for a big surprise, because you cannot be more wrong. It is the opposite; they get so much harder as you go along. The upside to this situation is that you will get smarter about the subjects. As you go through college, you will learn to be a better student. You know better ways to study and take tests and write papers. You also become more knowledgeable on the subjects that you are learning. In your junior year, you will be smarter in your major than in your first year. You get better at college every day because you learn from your mistakes and learn from the mistakes of others. You'll have some tough classes ahead, but you will get better at this whole college thing. Hopefully, in the end, you are good enough at college to keep up with those tough classes.

March 24th

"If you have much, give of your wealth; if you have little, give of your heart."

- Arab Proverb

While it is hard to think about now, we will all become much older one day, and eventually, we will not be on this earth anymore. For most of you reading this, that is many decades away, but it does beg the question: what mark do you want to leave here? Once you are gone, you are really gone. What you give back to the world is what you will be remembered for. Think of all of the things you can do now that will start leaving a mark on others. It could be helping some friends, or it could be donating to a local charity. As a college student, you probably do not have an abundance of money you can spend on others. Wealth can always be more than money. Some of the best wealth is knowledge. Passing down what you know to others is something that will outlive you. Kindness and love are other things people do not think of. You can pass that to friends and family, and it can be something of more value than money. You all have a while to live, but think about what you can do to give back to others.

March 25th

"A man is not called wise because he talks and talks again; but if he is peaceful, loving and fearless then he is in truth called wise."

- Buddha: Ancient Indian Religious Leader

You know that the person who is always talking is usually never saying anything worth listening to. It is easy to think that this person is smart because they have so much to say, but you will quickly find out that they might be the dumbest person you know. A great virtue of an intelligent person is that they are peaceful. They are not crazy, excited, or sad, but rather always very levelheaded and not overly worked up over anything. A calm person can make decisions because they have not let their emotions cloud their thoughts. They are also always very loving. These people never want to see anyone suffer and always show care to everyone they meet. A wise person also exhibits fearlessness. They have probably lived through several situations that were pretty terrifying. They have learned how to control themselves and not let fear overcome them. If you want to become wise, then peace, love, and fearlessness are the first virtues that you should try to embody.

March 26th

"Do not boast about tomorrow, for you do not know what a day may bring."

- Proverbs 27:1

Life is uncertain - that is why you cannot get too confident that you know what will happen tomorrow. You might be in a happy relationship today and be single tomorrow evening. You should not be taking everything that happens to you now for granted, because there is no guarantee that it will stay this way tomorrow. Many of you remember going to school like normal, and the next day a global pandemic begins. If you would have known that you would not be going back to school for the next year, you would have focused on enjoying that last day of school more. This just shows how quickly and unexpectedly the world around us can change. You should treat every day like you have no idea what will happen tomorrow. You have to realize you are a finite being, and everyone around you is too. Cherish the time you spend doing the things you love, with the people you love. Be thankful for the good things and the good people in your life because they will not always be there. We are not promised anything tomorrow, so enjoy it today.

March 27th

"You should always look on human life as short and cheap. Yesterday sperm; tomorrow a mummy or ashes."

- Marcus Aurelius: Roman Emperor & Stoic Philosopher

♦

Life is short. As someone in their early twenties, life seems to be pretty long still. However, you figure out from people around you that it is not. Tomorrow is not always guaranteed, so take advantage of today. There is no point in putting off doing what you have always wanted to; start today. Take the time to enjoy some of the smaller things in life; do not take them for granted. Go out with your friends, go talk to that person in class you always have wanted to, because life is too short to look back and wonder, *What if?* You have schoolwork, jobs, and other obligations. Do not throw those away to party every day, because that is not a better option. Do not spend all of your time studying, and do not spend all your time partying. Find the happy medium to where you can look back and think to yourself, *Wow, I really enjoyed that!* You do not have forever to live. Enjoy the fun of every activity that you partake in.

March 28th

"A man is but the product of his thoughts. What he thinks, he becomes."

- Mahatma Gandhi: 20th Century Indian Lawyer & Political Ethicist

◆

As you may know, you are not in control of many things in life. You are usually at the mercy of outside variables that determine what actions you will take. One of the few things you do have control over is your thoughts. Your thoughts are strictly your own. No one else can control what you think; this can be both a blessing and a curse. You are exactly how you feel. If you start thinking negative thoughts, negative outcomes are more likely to happen. Have you ever thought you would do badly at something, and you ended up doing pretty poorly? It is wrong to blame your thoughts, but how you feel does play a significant part in what happens. If you want to succeed at something, you have to start thinking that way. The more positive thoughts you can have, the more positive the outcomes of your actions will be. Sometimes it is hard not to doubt yourself, but this will negatively affect you. If you want to start seeing more positives in your life, start with your thoughts.

March 29th

"Judge a man by his questions rather than by his answers."

- Voltaire: 18th Century French Writer & Philosopher

Maybe the best thing you can do during your classes in college is to ask questions. Not only do your professors really enjoy this because it shows that you are paying attention, but it also helps you better understand the material. More than likely, someone else also has the same question as you, so you should not feel stupid for asking it. Never judge another person based on the questions that they ask. Questions help us work our way to the answers we are searching for. Another person might have a different way of getting to the answer than you do. Just because you might think that the question is dumb does not mean that the person asking it thinks it is. Questions show a genuine interest in the quest for knowledge. Answers might be a momentary solution to yet another question; new questions will help shape new answers. The person who asks questions in class is probably starting to grasp the material well. Do not judge a person for succeeding in their quest for proficiency in some subject.

March 30th

"Nothing is more honorable than a grateful heart."
- *Lucius Annaeus Seneca: Roman Stoic Philosopher*

Gratefulness is something that we could all learn to show a little more. Most of the time, we are so caught up in our lives and our problems that we do not take enough time to step back and see what others actually do for us. It is sad to see someone do so much for another person. While that other person only focuses on the bad that the other may do. It is easy to sit there and say that someone did not do enough for you. However, if you take a step back and look at everything they do, you realize just how much good they do. Being grateful for what others do rather than being so negative to only see the bad is one of the greatest things a person can do. Feeling grateful not only makes you a better person, but it makes you actually feel better too. Studies show that people who exhibit more gratefulness are happier. Remember to always be grateful for what others do for you. Even if it is something small, they did it out of the kindness of their heart. The least you can do is be grateful for that.

March 31st

"If there is no wind, row."

- Latin Proverb

In high school, you usually had most of your decisions made for you. Someone else decided when you would go to class and do your extracurricular activities. The teachers made sure you turned in your homework, and your family made sure you did your homework. Someone was always the wind to your boat. They always made sure you were sailing forward. When you go to college, everything changes. All of a sudden, you have to be your own wind. You are not totally on your own, but more than you ever have been before. No one is making sure that you do your homework or turn it in. No one is scheduling your day for you. All of these things are stuff you have to do on your own. You might not have any wind blowing your boat. You might not have any momentum to do the things you normally do. In this case, the only choice that you have is to row. You may not want to do your homework today, but you have to find some motivation to do it. Things you do not feel like doing will always be abundant. You just have to row through it.

April

April 1st

"Is your reputation bothering you? Remember how soon we are all forgotten. The abyss of endless time swallows us all."

- Marcus Aurelius: Roman Emperor & Stoic Philosopher

We all know what it feels like when a friend or ex talks badly behind your back and spreads untrue rumors that make you sound like a jerk. It seems like everyone you know is looking at you differently, like you are a bad person. Or maybe you actually did something to ruin your own reputation. Either way, while it sucks now, give it some time, and you will see that people will either forget or forgive and move on. There is no need to run around trying to explain yourself to everyone that you know. People like to gossip, and there is hardly anything you can do to stop the rumors that are spread. We are all going to be gone one day, and all of those rumors and untrue statements will vanish in time. Take it one day at a time. It might be rough for a couple of days, but it will get better sooner than you think. Your reputation will soon rebound from these problems. Just remember that no rumor or gossip about you is going to stick around forever.

April 2nd

"And speak to people kindly."
- Surah Baqarah Ayat 83

Too often, we speak to others inappropriately. We often talk to people in ways we would not like to be talked to. Maybe we are too often busy trying to get everything done and feel rushed or overwhelmed. We almost forget that the person we are talking to is another human being. We can all think of a time when we have been yelled at for no reason. If you look at who yelled at you and the day they had, you can probably understand why they were upset. It is often because they are overwhelmed or irritated, and you happened to be the person they took it out on. See, you remembered a time when someone talked to you unkindly; it is something that can stick with us for a long time. Think about all the times you have spoken unkindly to someone; the way you snapped at them is probably something they can still remember. The best way to avoid these problems is to talk to everyone like you would like to be talked to. Treat others with respect, especially in the way you speak to them.

April 3rd

"The only true wisdom is in knowing you know nothing."
- Socrates: Ancient Greek Philosopher

◆

No one likes a know-it-all; they come off as arrogant, pretentious, and rude. Why would you want to spend time with someone with those qualities? Something equally sad is that some people reach a certain age and decide to stop learning. They think they know enough to get by because they have hit this certain age (even though they probably do not know enough). There will come a time when you stop going to school. For some, it is when they are eighteen; others might be well into their thirties. No matter what your age, never stop seeking out knowledge. You might think you know a lot, but you have only grazed the top. Ask questions and try new things. You do not have to be in a classroom to learn. There is always something new to learn. Do not be the person who graduates and then thinks that they are above learning something new. The more you learn, the more people you get to know, and you become more interesting. It never hurts to have some new tricks in the bag either.

April 4th

"We will either find a way or make one."
- Hannibal: Cartesian General & Statesman

It is really hard to keep going when you hit the wall with your schoolwork. There comes a time for us when we are mentally burned out, and it is a real struggle to do anything productive in our classes. It often happens more than any of us would like to admit. This is the time in the semester when your grades can really drop if you do not remain diligent with your work. People can have really good grades and then hit the point of burnout and have to work to not fail those classes. Your parents and family might just tell you, "You got this" and "Do your best," but that does not really help your feeling of not wanting to do any more schoolwork. The best advice is to just ride the wave. You will hit this low point, and if you can just try to do the minimum amount of work to do well, then do that until you start to feel better. The worst thing you can do is try to put more time and effort in when you feel burnt out; it leads to faster burnout. Take your time and just pace yourself. It will pass, and you will recover.

April 5th

"Speak well of your friend; of your enemy, neither well nor ill."

- Italian Proverb

Very rarely will you gain an enemy for life. You might have someone on your bad side for a while, but you probably will not have a lifetime enemy. Regardless of your relationship with anyone, you really should refrain from speaking badly about them. You definitely should not talk badly about your friends because they are your friends. How would you like it if one of your closest friends talked badly behind your back? So why do that to them? It is easy to bad-mouth someone you do not like because they did something bad to you. In fact, they might even deserve to have some dirt on their reputation. This will only be bad for you. Somehow, they will find out, and you will just ruin your relationship with that person even more. There is no point in destroying relationships, even if they deserve it. You have to be the bigger person, move on, and leave them be. It might not be the most fun thing to do, but it is right. You might not have an enemy, but if you talk badly about people enough, you just might gain one. Talk about others how you would want to be talked about.

April 6th

"Live in the sunshine, swim in the sea, drink the wild air."

- Ralph Waldo Emerson: 19th Century American Philosopher

◆

Chances are that when you go to college, you will be in a different town with different people. You are going to get moved into your new dorm room or apartment. Your family will soon leave, and it is just you and your roommates. Now, you could stay in your room all day except to go to class, work on homework, and lie in your bed. How fun will that be to think back on? That sounds like a very dull college experience. Or you can make this time a new adventure in your life. You can explore the college town you are in and find all the new fun spots to go to. You can learn new hobbies that you have always wanted to try out. You can go explore campus and see all it has to offer. There is no limit to new things that you can do. Does this not sound like a much more exciting and interesting college experience? You are free to enjoy the wonders that life gives you. Every day is a new experience to be lived. Enjoy this time with your friends, and do new fun things, because this is a life worth living.

April 7th

"Without labor, nothing prospers."
- *Sophocles: Ancient Greek Tragedian*

Whether you want to be a successful student, athlete, or employee, you will have to work for it. You will never have success given to you for no reason; it is earned. All good things happen because of hard work. Suppose you want to have a successful college career as a student. In that case, you will have to work each semester at mastering your classes while branching out and meeting new people. Suppose you want to have success as a student athlete. In that case, you will have to work at maintaining and keeping up with your classes and mastering your game in your designated sport. If you want to be a successful employee, you will have to work at being the best in your field. No matter what you are doing, if you're going to start to see successes in your life, you will need to work at it. In personal relationships, you will have to be a good friend or partner. It does not matter what you are doing. Work hard at it, and you will start to reap the benefits from the success you get.

April 8th

"Even if you're going to live three thousand more years, or ten times that, remember: you cannot lose another life than the one you're living now, or live another one than the one you're losing."

- Marcus Aurelius: Roman Emperor & Stoic Philosopher

♦

Even though you are going to college to further your education and get a diploma to get a good job, you cannot forget to enjoy it while you are there. We do not really know how long we have here on earth. You have one life here, and you cannot take it for granted. Do not forget to go out and enjoy life. Go out with friends or do the hobbies that bring you joy. Go seek activities that you would have never thought of doing, because college is a great time to figure yourself out and find what you love. Not everything you try will be something you find fun, but that is okay. At least you now know and will not regret trying it. Sometimes we get so caught up with our grades, or the next quiz or test, that we do not take the time to enjoy life. You should also learn to enjoy the process of learning. You will probably not go to college again, so enjoy every class because this might be the last time you do it.

April 9th

"He is a man of courage who does not run away, but remains at his post and fights against the enemy."

- Socrates: Ancient Greek Philosopher

We, as humans, have an instinct to avoid problems. Whenever there is a problem, we often try to distance ourselves from it. Why do you run from your problems? What is running away going to help? All you have done is momentarily postponed the inevitable of dealing with it. It is always better to not run but to deal with the issues head-on. Facing whatever problems or fears you have will only help you. When we go through hard times, we get stronger. You will become a much stronger person when you walk away from this situation than you did coming into it. Whether it is school problems or social life issues, putting off dealing with it will only worsen the case for both you and everyone involved. Build up some courage and deal with it. If for no other reason, at least it gets the problem over with sooner. You are much stronger than you think you are, and you can face whatever you are going through. No more running from your problems; it is time to face them.

April 10th

"Set your heart on doing good. Do it over and over again, and you will be filled with joy."

- Buddha: Ancient Indian Religious Leader

Hopefully, you have the drive to help others in life. Maybe you are choosing your major with the hope of helping people in your future. There are people whose main reason for choosing the major they did was to help them have the opportunity to help people. Even now, you can help others. It may be something small like holding the door or helping your roommate clean the apartment. You can also help in bigger ways like volunteering. Whatever it is, hopefully there is something inside of you that wants to help others. Maybe some of you just do not have the want to help others. That is okay. Not everyone has that drive. If you do not feel this, all that can be asked is that you do not do bad. We are all different and have different values. Some have a driving call to do good in others' lives, while some do not have this. All that can be asked from both parties is that you try not to do bad things in others' lives.

April 11th

"He will win who knows when to fight and when not to fight."

- Sun Tzu: Ancient Chinese Military Strategist & Philosopher

There are just times in life when it is best to let things go. Are you really going to accomplish anything by arguing with your partner over every single little problem in the relationship? Or is finals week really the best time to confront your roommate about the dishes that they left in the sink? Most of the time, it is just going to lead to more problems than there were before the arguments. Most arguments and disagreements are not worth the pain that is felt after. It is always good to figure out when and when not to bring up a problem. Whether it be friends, family, significant others, or anyone else. There are just times when it is best to let it go and move on. Unless you are sure what you are about to bring up is going to be for the greater good of the relationship, it might be best to just brush it aside and carry on. There is no problem with walking away from some things. Fight the fights worth fighting for, lift your chin, and move on when they are not worth it.

April 12th

"Only the educated are free."
- *Epictetus: Ancient Greek Philosopher*

College is not for everyone. This is not saying that you have to go to college or continue to go to school to live your best life. You can graduate college, go straight into the workforce, and continue to be educated. The education you receive does not have to be in a classroom setting. Some of the best lessons you may learn in your life will not happen in school. These lessons are learning opportunities. You should always be open to learning. You should learn to listen, explore, and question ideas. You can do all of this without ever stepping foot in a classroom. When you continue to learn, you open up your mind to new ideas and thoughts. This is a very liberating feeling. We have all been there before when you learn something, and your mind is absolutely blown. When you are learning something you are so interested that you are drawn into the subject and absolutely love it. If you can mentally be liberated by learning something, that is one of the most basic freedoms you can have.

April 13th

"Do not withhold good from those to whom it is due, when it is in your power to act."

- Proverbs 3:27

Try to always bring good into your life and the lives of others around you. You always have the power to do good for others. If you can help your family with something, then go help. You do not always need to physically give something to someone else to help. Just a few simple words of affirmation to someone close to you can really bring happiness into their life. We all wonder if what we are doing is the smart option or the right move. Just letting someone know that they are doing good can help their spirits out. If you are not doing something for someone else because you do not feel like doing it, you are withholding joy and happiness from that person's life. It is wrong to withhold good deeds from someone. If someone kept joy from you, I bet you would be pretty frustrated. Joy is one of those things that everyone needs more of in their life. Why would you withhold it from others if you would not like to have it withheld from you? Give them the happiness that they deserve.

April 14th

"Philosophy teaches us to act, not speak."
- Lucius Annaeus Seneca: Roman Stoic Philosopher

Whether you are interested in philosophy or not, there are still lessons that you can learn from it. One of the greatest lessons you can learn is that action speaks louder than words. Many people talk about what they want to accomplish; few actually follow through and do it. You will find many people who will tell you what they want to major in, what job they want, and all these different future goals. However, that is just talking; it takes a lot more to actually go out and accomplish those goals. Many people talk about other things they want to do or what they want to be well before they know how to actually do it. Do not be this person. There are times when you just need to go work for your dreams and not say a word. Would you rather talk about having a college degree and good life or actually have it? Obtaining your goals and being able to enjoy your success is much more enjoyable than just talking about them. The most successful people do not talk about being successful; they just go out and do it.

April 15th

"Failing to understand the workings of ones' own mind is bound to lead to unhappiness."

- Marcus Aurelius: Roman Emperor & Stoic Philosopher

It is no secret that each of us is unique and different. That means that there is no one-size-fits-all solution to happiness. While some solutions work for some, they do not work for others. Part of this quest to find peace and happiness is to look inward to your own mind. You have to start realizing how you work. If you do not know how you work, then how will you know what will make you happy? Spend some time with yourself, and take the time to look upon your own mind and find out who you really are. College is a very busy time in your life. Taking the time to find out about yourself is probably not making the list of top 100 things to do. However, you do not want to spend some of the best years of your life being miserable. You are in a time in life when you are constantly evolving. What you liked last year may no longer be something you like now. Take just a little bit of time each day to get to know yourself, and you will become a happier person.

April 16th

"The way you make your bed, is the way you shall lie."
— Swedish Proverb

A big part of growing up is learning to accept the consequences of your own actions. Before college, you could get away with many different things, and you usually had little to no repercussions. Now that you are an adult, you are held more accountable for your actions. If you did not study for a test, you cannot go to your professor and use some excuse to get out of it. If you are there, they will make you take it and often do not care how you do. The consequences of which are probably going to be pretty unpleasant. Failing at something is never fun, but it is often a necessary consequence of your actions. It teaches you that if you do not want to feel this pain again, you will have to do something different. It sounds weird to say that the bad consequences are good, but they often are. It awakens you to the problems that you need to fix. The water in the ship is not good, but it shows you where the holes are that you need to patch. You will have to learn to live with the consequences of your own actions; they will help you figure out what you need to do better.

April 17th

"Another person cannot hurt you without your cooperation; you are hurt the moment you believe yourself to be."

- Marcus Aurelius: Roman Emperor & Stoic Philosopher

In life, we are bound to get hurt. It is almost impossible to never be hurt in some way. We can feel pain physically, mentally, emotionally, and spiritually. What is sad is that other people can inflict pain in all of those categories. However, everyone can overcome these obstacles and the pain they will inevitably encounter. A great way to do this is to focus on not letting what others say and do affect how you feel. This is something that is obviously easier said than done. If you can concentrate on not letting what others say about you affect you or what others think of you affect how you see yourself, then you have won. If someone talks badly behind your back, and you let those words upset and anger you, you have hurt yourself the moment you accept what they say. However, if you do not let what others say get under your skin; you have not let the actions of others hurt you. Focus on not letting the actions and words of others affect how you see yourself, and go about your life.

April 18th

"First say to yourself what you would be; and then do what you have to do."

- Epictetus: Ancient Greek Philosopher

Now you have finally hit the point in your life where you actually get to start to really think about what you want to be in life. Sure, we have all thought about what we wanted to be when we grew up, but now is when it starts becoming a reality. The really cool thing about this decision is that you can become anything you want to be. So, what is it you want to be? It is one thing to say what you want to be. It is another thing to do it. If you're going to be a doctor, you are really going to have to want to be a doctor. With whatever you wish to pursue, you will make some major time and effort commitments to that subject. Once you choose your calling, you need to buckle down and do what you have to do to get it. If that means taking some summer classes, then do it. If it means not going out in order to focus on studying, then do that. Do what you have to do to succeed. This will be your calling for the rest of your life, so do what needs to be done to accomplish that.

April 19th

"Good decisions come from experience. Experience comes from making bad decisions."
- Mark Twain: 19th Century American Writer

We do not always make the best decisions. In fact, college students are known for not making great decisions. From a bad decision comes experience, and that experience helps us to make better decisions the next time. When you make the bad decision to skip class for a week straight, you are going to get some experience out of it. It may come in the form of a poor exam or quiz grade. It could also be that you do not understand a basic concept that will be used for the rest of the semester. Whatever the consequences are, you will have to live with them and move on. There is some good that comes from this though. You now know that if you skip class, you are going to do poorly on a test or struggle to understand the material for the rest of the semester. This experience of doing poorly at something will help you to make better decisions in the future. The upshot for you is that a bad decision now is knowing how to do it better in the future.

April 20th

"It does not matter how slowly you go as long as you do not stop."

- Confucius: Ancient Chinese Philosopher

There is always a lot of pressure to go to college and walk out of there with a diploma in four years or less. From taking college classes in high school, to loading up on courses on summer and winter breaks. Students are doing everything in their power to try to graduate in the shortest amount of time possible. Sure, college is expensive, and you do not want to pay for more than you need. However, if it takes you five years to graduate, it is equally as impressive of a feat. Do not get discouraged that you are not keeping pace with your peers. As long as you are working away and knocking out all the classes you need, if it ends up being an extra semester or two, that is totally fine. The worst thing you could do is to give up. As long as you do not give up because you get upset that you are not going as fast as your classmates. In the long run, as long as you have your diploma, even if it took you an extra year, it does not matter. This goes for all your goals that you will have in life. As long as you keep going and never stop, it will all work out in the end.

April 21st

"It is not enough to learn how to ride, you must also learn how to fall."

- Mexican Proverb

Part of learning how to succeed is learning how to fail. You might think to yourself, Why would I want to fail? Well, if you never fail, then you never know what success really is. It is like how you cannot have darkness without light. You need some of one thing to understand and experience the other. Hopefully, you have success in everything that you pursue, you will encounter some failures from time to time. You will fail at something in your classes, but that makes your success even better. You will have letdowns at making friends, but it makes the ones you have that much better. You will not have success in every relationship you get into. However, it is going to make finding the one that much sweeter. Failures suck, sure, but they are necessary to learn from them to make sure that they do not happen again, making success that much sweeter. We all know the feeling of having success at something we failed at previously; it feels pretty good. Do not wish to never have failures; rather, try to overcome failures so you can really enjoy success.

April 22nd

"There is advantage in the wisdom won from pain."
- Aeschylus: Ancient Greek Tragedian

Oh, how we wish that pain would go away forever. Pain is never something anyone is just super excited to experience, but it is a necessary experience. There is a type of personal growth that comes from pain. From physical pain, we become physically strong. The same can be said for other aspects of life. If you feel mental pain from studying all day, you will become mentally stronger. Think about who you were ten years ago. You probably were not very tough, nor were you very smart. You have gained a certain amount of knowledge about life. Most of this knowledge came from some sort of pain. You learned to wear a helmet when you crashed your bike. Why? Because it really hurt when you smacked your head on the concrete. Just as you know, be careful who you let into your life, because it really hurts when they leave. As painful as those experiences were, you gained a certain amount of wisdom and knowledge from them. Do not be upset when you are dealt with an unfortunate situation because it will make you a stronger and wiser person.

April 23rd

"What upsets people is not things themselves, but their judgement about these things."

- Epictetus: Ancient Greek Philosopher

Life gives us plenty of unfavorable outcomes. Many people's college experiences have been less than favorable. Probably the main reason would be the global pandemic that caused many to miss out on the in-person life of college for almost two years. That is half of one's college undergraduate experience that is just gone. Sure, you can be upset with that, as many are with the situation. You can look at this situation of your college experience and be pretty upset with all that got messed up for you and the rest of the world. That is only my individual judgment of the situation though. Judgments can be changed. You can judge this situation as bad and be upset about it. However, what are you going to accomplish looking at something in that way? Or you can look at it as an opportunity to grow and learn self-discipline and really focus on school. A situation may not be as bad as what you think it is. You just have to have a different view of it.

April 24th

"Dream no small dreams for they have no power to move the hearts of people."

- Johann Wolfgang Von Goethe: 18th Century German Poet & Playwright

---

You have big dreams that you want to complete one day. We all have some big goals that we want to achieve. It is sad to hear how people will give up on their dreams because they just do not think they are realistic enough. These people have given up on themselves and their ideas before attempting them. All of our futures will be how we want to pursue our dreams. Do not give up on your dreams, even if they seem unrealistic. The least you can do is begin to pursue your goals and then take them from there. You might be surprised at how obtainable your goal actually was. You need to believe that you can achieve your dreams. Make goals for yourself and set out a plan to follow for achieving those dreams. If you truly believe in yourself, there is no limit to what you will accomplish. Great things come to those with great dreams. There will be failures and some low points, but if you can persevere through these low points, you will be able to reap the benefits of your success.

April 25th

"it is courage, courage, courage, that raises the blood of life to crimson splendor. Live bravely and present a brave front to adversity."

- Horace: Ancient Roman Lyric Poet

There are no ends of things that can intimidate a new college student. Choosing the right major, making friends, homesickness, and stressful classes are just a few of the challenges that new college students may face. It can be pretty easy to let the pressures of these new issues get the best of you. In order to not crumble under the pressure, you must have courage. When you are trying to choose the right major, people will tell you what you should and should not study. Only you know what is best for you and your goals in life. It takes courage to choose the major that is best for you and disregard what others will tell you. In order to make new friends in college, you have to go out and talk to new people. Approaching new people requires a certain amount of bravery and courage. It takes courage to know that going away to college is the best thing for you. It is always a bit scary to venture into the unknown of college. Have the courage and bravery to step into that unknown.

April 26th

"I find that the harder I work, the more luck I seem to have."

- Thomas Jefferson: 3rd President of the United States

It is always nice when we get lucky with some situation. When there is a pop quiz over something you have no idea about, and you pass, it feels good when you have luck on your side. If you want to have more chances, just work more. Luck and hard work go hand in hand. The harder you work, the luckier you will be. Usually, the more work you put in, the more things end up going your way. When you study for a test for hours, and then are stuck on a question on the test, you might get lucky and have the answer pop in your head. Maybe you can call it luck, or maybe you can say that the amount of time you prepared helped. While luck might show up once or twice when you are unprepared, it will be more abundant when you are ready. So, if you need some luck on your side, go put in the work, and it will show up when you need it. You might be surprised how much luck you have when you are well prepared for whatever you are doing.

April 27th

"Do not let the future trouble you. You will come to it (if that is what you must) possessed of the same reason that you apply now to the present."

- Marcus Aurelius: Roman Emperor & Stoic Philosopher

School becomes a lot more stressful once you get to college. Sure, you have more freedom and more interesting classes than high school. However, these classes hold higher standards than your high school classes. If you strive for academic excellence, then you put even more pressure on yourself. The most stressful times in college fall around when you have tests. Professors are generally nice enough to give you a sizeable notice of when your test will be. Now you have this future date that you are studying for. At some point, you will probably get tired and overwhelmed and start to doubt yourself. If you are preparing for the test now, you should have no reason to worry about this future test. Suppose you can go about studying and preparing for it calmly. In that case, you should take the examination the same way. Worrying about an upcoming test does nothing to help you prepare. Keeping calm and getting prepared will help you immensely when it is time to take the test.

April 28th

"Nothing is miserable unless you think it so; and on the other hand, nothing brings happiness unless you are content with it."

- Boethius: Roman Senator & Philosopher

We often label a situation as good or bad depending on how feelings are about it. A day where you have nothing on and can relax all day is usually viewed as good. An exam worth 30 percent of your final grade is not good. Are these situations good or bad, or is it just that our perception is good or bad? That exam is worth a big percentage of your final grade, which probably brings you some anxiety. It is also a big test, which you are not looking forward to. One could go out on a limb and say that your judgment of the exam is not good. The test itself is not bad. It is just your perception of it. If you changed your attitude about it, it might not be as bad as you imagine. Going in excited rather than dreading it will help you think more positively about it, just like the day filled with nothing but relaxation. It is not a good or bad day, but your judgment of it is what makes it good. You have the power to turn any situation better if you think of it in a more positive light.

April 29th

"Life without experience and suffering is not life."
- Socrates: Ancient Greek Philosopher

There would be no good without bad. How would you know if something is good if you never experienced the bad? Life has its ups and downs. You never truly live life without this roller coaster of positive and negative events. If you pass every class with no issues and get a job without any problems and then live the rest of your life with absolutely zero issues, this is pretty lame. At first, it sounds like the best option, but think about it for a second. Would you really like to live that boring life, where every morning you wake up and you know nothing interesting is going to happen? Sure, bad things suck, but at least they make life a bit more interesting. It absolutely sucks to get heartbroken, but you gain experience and pain. The pain helps you realize the mistake and not make it again. As much as we would all like bad things to go away, they are pretty helpful in our lives, and plus, they add some excitement. Looking back at the bad, you will at least be able to say that you lived a full life.

April 30th

"Curb your desires – don't set your heart on so many things and you will get what you need."

- Epictetus: Ancient Greek Philosopher

It is noticeable for undergraduate students, especially freshmen, that they think they have their lives figured out. They majored in what they have wanted to study since being little, and they will get this very specific job in a very specific town. They have their heart set on all these goals, and then boom. They realize they do not like their major or do not like what jobs they can get. Whatever it may be, they know that all these "wants" that they had their heart set on are no longer things they want anymore. It is never a bad thing to change your major. Better to do it now than realize it twenty years from now. When you first start college, just take it one step at a time. Really, depending on your college, you do not have to worry about what you want to major in your first year. You have so many prerequisite and core classes that everyone has to take. Figure out what you want to study first, then let all the rest come as it does. There is no reason to get ahead of yourself.

May

May 1st

"I begin to speak only when I'm certain what I'll say isn't better left unsaid."

- Cato: Roman Senator

Whether in an argument with a friend, family member, or significant other, it is best to just sometimes not speak. You may see someone try to explain themselves or tell the other person how to think in an argument, which leads to disaster. We have all been the victim of this fault at one point or another. Before you say something in a fight, ask yourself, "Is what I am about to say going to benefit me in this argument to help clear the situation up?" If the answer is no, it is best not to say it. In most arguments you will encounter, you and the other person are against the problem, not you versus them. You are trying to clean up an issue with a relationship, not trying to hurt the other person. People often talk just to hear themselves talk; some of what they say is not valuable information. It is best to speak less and only speak when you can contribute helpful and uplifting ideas, not break down others.

May 2nd

"There is no substitute for hard work in winning success."

- James J. Hill: 19th Century Canadian-American Railroad Director

---

As we all know, an elevator will get you where you need to go in a building easier and with less physical stress. When given a choice, most people will take an elevator rather than the stairs. You could think of success like the top floor of a very old building. There is no elevator to that top floor. You have to take the stairs. Success requires time and effort, just as the stairs do. There is no way to succeed if you put minimal effort and time into it. Just think about it: if you do not study or do any reading for a class, do you think you will have success in that class? You can go out on a limb and say probably not. It is no secret that success comes from hard work. People might tell you shortcuts they might think work to succeed faster. Still, usually, none of these shortcuts actually work. Suppose you are serious about having success in whatever you want. In that case, you will have to put some serious time and effort into it. Do not look for an easy way out, because there is no easy way to succeed. There is no way to push a button and ride to the top. You are going to have to climb for it.

May 3rd

"Life is really simple, but we insist on making it complicated."
- *Confucius: Ancient Chinese Philosopher*

Really when you think about it, college is not that hard. At least on paper, it is not that hard. You just go to class, do your work, wake up, and do it again. There are a lot of other factors that do not make it that simple. Sometimes it feels like we almost try to make things complicated when we just need to think of the simplest solution. You are going to college to get a degree. That should be priority number one. Doing activities to eliminate burnout is number two. Whether seeing friends or playing basketball for a couple of hours, whatever helps clear your mind and supports your mental health. So really, you just need to go to class and study and keep your mental health up. It is easier said than done, but it does not have to be super complicated. There is no super complex solution to college. Just go to class, keep your mental health up, and everything else should fall into place. We often overthink what we need to do. Most of the answers we need are either right in front of us or take little effort to find. Life is not super complicated, so do not make it harder than it needs to be.

May 4th

"Little strokes fell great oaks."
- Benjamin Franklin: 18th Century Writer & Inventor

When we were younger, we all did some activity that we really wanted to have success in. Maybe you were big into sports, or perhaps it was music. Think of the first time you picked up a ball or a musical instrument. Chances are, you were pretty bad at playing them. You enjoyed the activity enough that you spent countless hours practicing. You practiced dribbling the basketball for hours and always tried to perfect your shot. Or you sat in your room looking over sheet music, trying to get your instrument to sound just right. All those hours of practice seem pretty small in hindsight. However, no matter how small the hours of training seemed, they added up, and you got pretty good at your activity. You can apply this same story to anything you are doing in life. If you want to succeed in college, you have to spend some time doing the little things. You will have to study and read to get better at retaining the information. You will get out of something that you put into it, so put in the work, and you will see success.

May 5th

"A person who won't read has no advantage over one who can't read."

- Mark Twain: 19th Century American Writer

A big reason you are going to college is to do something later on with that degree. Maybe you want to go into healthcare and help others. Or you want to go into engineering and change the way humanity does something. Whatever you want to do, your education is the bridge to it. The work you put into your education today will be what you can do with your life later on. Suppose you want to be a doctor and save lives in the future. In that case, you need to take that chemistry class seriously, so you can apply those fundamental concepts to more advanced ones eventually in medical school. Those mathematics classes will help you with future engineering projects down the road. What you learn now will be helpful for you at some point down the road. Do not neglect the classes you are taking now and write them off as unimportant. These classes are what will make you into what you want to be. Most of these classes will be the stepping-stones to the pathway of your future goals.

May 6th

"It is impossible to live a pleasant life without living wisely and well and justly."

- Epictetus: Ancient Greek Philosopher

When you were about to go off to college, at least one person will tell you to, "make good decisions." You most likely smiled and said you would and brushed it off. However, this is more important than you think. When you are at college, you are never more than one unwise decision away from doing something that will turn your life into a pretty bad one. If you are out partying and decide to get behind the wheel, you very well might have made a bad decision that will lead to a life that is anything but pleasant. That being said, it is impossible to always make good decisions, and mistakes happen. You just have to make sure that you think about the long-term consequences of your actions. Going out to party when you have a test the next morning is probably not the wisest decision. Still, it will not lead to an unpleasant life forever. It might lead to a tough week after or even a tough semester, but you will live. Just make sure you think through whether this decision will positively affect everyone.

May 7th

"The best revenge is to be unlike he who performed the injury."

- Marcus Aurelius: Roman Emperor & Stoic Philosopher

In your life, you will start to see a lot of people change. Some of it is because your peers are coming to an age where their circumstances make them change. It can also be because you are older now and not as naïve. You now see things as maybe an adult would see them rather than as a kid does. This means you will see people do you wrong. Whether it be friends going behind your back or significant others who talk badly about you when you're not around. Unfortunately, it can even be family members who no longer support you. Whatever it is, there will be times when you are filled with anger or hatred toward another person, and you feel the need to get them back for what they did to you. You should take a moment and realize that revenge will not help. All you will do is create this sort of loop between you and someone else, always getting revenge on each other. Is this what you want? The best way to go about it is simply not to do what they have done to you. What better way to show your maturity than to not react?

May 8th

"The most beautiful fig may contain a worm."
- African Proverb

College might be the first time you get into a romantic relationship with someone. Being in a relationship with someone is always a special time in your life. Love is a powerful feeling; sometimes, it is too powerful. It is easy to overlook another person's flaws when you are in love with them. This can lead to some issues down the line for yourself. You might be blinded by love and being in a new relationship where you don't know the problems that the other person can cause. They might seem like good-looking, nice, caring people, but on the inside, they do not have the best interest of both of you at heart. It might sometimes seem like your friends, and even your family, always find the bad in the person you are dating. While some of it might just be them giving you a bad time, you also should listen to what they are saying. You do not want other people to use you rather than love you. It might hurt for a bit if the relationship ends, but it allows you to look and see that the person may not have been all you thought they were.

May 9th

"Everything you have ever wanted is on the other side of fear."

- George Addair: 19th Century American Real Estate Developer

◆

The real world is scary. College is your first real glimpse at what the real world is like. You are on your own, and you are the one calling the shots. It can be pretty scary going to a five-hundred-person lecture. It can also be rather frightening to give a presentation in front of twenty people. There is no shortage of fears you might encounter in your first experiences in college and the real world. These fears can be debilitating. There are people who would not go to class because they were scared to give a presentation or just talk to other people. It is pretty hard to pass your classes if you do not show up because of fear. If you want to graduate and get that diploma and a good job down the road, you are going to have to face your fears now. The things that you want often require you to go through some sort of fear. If you do not, then all those dreams of yours down the road that require you to pass this class all of a sudden no longer exist. Face those fears, and you will see that you are capable of more than you think.

May 10th

"To dare is to lose one's footing momentarily. To not dare is to lose oneself."

- Soren Kierkegaard: 18th century Danish Philosopher

Sometimes you will not see the path you need to walk in life. It is not that you have lost your way and are off the course; it just sometimes requires that you take a brief step into the unknown to get back on the seen path. Every step of your goals will not be fully set out; you will have to take a daring unknown action a few times to keep going. If you never dare to take that novel step, then you will never live. You can always stay on the lighted path, but it only takes you so far in life. Taking this step in the dark will often make you feel like you might fall. Everything is so unknown that you do not know if you are right or wrong. Sure, it is a bit of a limbo, but you will come out the other side better than you were before. If you never take that step, you will never find your way. You might not always know what you are about to step into in life. Whether it is school, a job, or your social life, you will have times when you feel lost. This feeling will only last momentarily because that step will set you on the right path. Never taking that step will leave you in the same place you are now.

May 11th

"As long as you live keep learning how to live; to err is human, but to persist (in the mistake) is diabolical."

- Lucius Annaeus Seneca: Roman Stoic Philosopher

Most of us associate making a mistake with something bad. This is probably because the consequences of the error were not something you enjoyed. However, making mistakes is one of the simplest ways of learning. You should see this as an opportunity to learn and become better. Sure, the consequences of some errors are awful, but you will move on, and you have learned to not do that again. The more severe the effects, the less likely you will make that mistake again. Sometimes, we will make a mistake and not learn from it. This is not good for many reasons. One of the main ones is that you will continually suffer the same consequences over and over. How often are you going to get told off by your professors or get into an argument with a significant other before you realize your mistakes? We are all going to make mistakes; you just have to make sure you learn something from them. A single mistake can be forgiven. Repeating the same error just means you are not thinking.

May 12th

"How long are you going to wait before you demand the best of yourself?"

- Epictetus: Ancient Greek Philosopher

If you really wanted to, you could go through life by just getting by. You could do just enough to get your high school degree, then do just enough to get a college degree, and just enough to get a job supporting your family. There really is nothing stopping you from becoming completely average and doing the bare minimum to get by in life. But what is the fun of living like that? There is something inside of you that wants to be the best. We all have a little competitive drive inside us, wanting to succeed. It does not matter if you have been going through life with mediocracy, but today is the day that you can change that. You can try a little harder in schoolwork and a little harder at your job. You can be a better person by just having the mindset to become better. Once you make this decision and really focus on doing the best you possibly can, you will start to notice an increase in every area of your life. Your grades will be better, your job will get better, and most importantly, you will be happier. Sure, it will be tougher, but the feeling of accomplishment is so much more rewarding.

May 13th

"Life's like a play: it's not the length, but the excellence of the acting that matters."

- Lucius Annaeus Seneca: Roman Stoic Philosopher

We all have something that we would like to be excellent at. Some of us want to be exceptional students. Others want to be outstanding athletes. In contrast, others want to be excellent workers, business owners, etc. If you really want to be excellent, you need to look at what you are doing and determine if it is enough to be considered excellent. If you're going to be an outstanding student, are you giving your all in every single class and maybe doing more than is asked of you? If you want to be an excellent athlete, are you going to those optional workouts and giving your best effort every rep? An outstanding worker and business owner is doing all that they can to contribute to the company as much as they can. If you cannot say that you do excellent work, you will never get better. Now, this does not mean that you cannot end up becoming better. You just need to change your habits. Start by giving outstanding effort toward each thing you do, and if you do this, you will become excellent at your craft.

May 14th

"What is done well is done quickly enough."
- *Augustus: First Roman Emperor*

There is a fine line between getting something done well and on time and something done and on time. You will be on both opposing poles of this in college. You will write a really great and thorough paper, but it took about three weeks of constant revisions and rewrites. You will also knock a paper out in about an hour just to get it in before the deadline. That paper did not get the same fine-tooth comb that the other did. You should try to strive for the first paper than the second. It might not be the quickest task, but it will produce the best quality. You have to start relating time and quality. The faster something is done, there is a higher probability that it will not be as good. Sometimes, the price you pay for having something done well is a little extra time. It is easy to rush through things just to get them done and turned in. However, that task is riddled with mistakes and issues since you hurried through it. This principle can be related to anything in your life. If you are going to do something, you might as well do it well. Slow down and do a thorough job on it, and you will see better results.

May 15th

"Change in all things is sweet."
- Aristotle: Ancient Greek Philosopher

Bad things are always going to be around in everyone's life. We are all going to experience some bad things. These bad things will not be fun and are most likely just going to downright suck. The good news is that there is a ray of light at the end of the tunnel. Some of the best things in life happen after a bad thing. You are going to get heartbroken. You felt like that person was the one; they told you that you were the one. You loved them, and you thought that they loved you too. The next thing you know, they are in bed with someone else, and you are crying in yours. There is no way to sugarcoat it; this sucks. You will soon realize that they were not who you thought they were. Now that you are back on the market, you might meet the person you were meant to be with. If you are going through a breakup, you might not think that there is anyone there for you. Give yourself some time to heal, and you will soon find the person who was ten times better than your ex ever could have been.

May 16th

"If you hear a voice within you say, 'you cannot paint,' then by all means paint, and that voice will be silenced."

- Vincent Van Gogh: 19th Century Dutch Painter

Something we will all face at one time or another is self-doubt. Some will have these thoughts more than others, but we all go through it. Doubting yourself is one of the quickest ways to kill any goal. If you think that you cannot do something, you immediately stop. A great way to counteract this is to do exactly what those thoughts tell you that you cannot do. If you think that you cannot go to college because you doubt you are smart enough, then go to class every day and prove yourself wrong. Those self-doubts will quickly go away when you start proving to yourself that you can do what you thought you could not. You feel that even your mind is telling you that you cannot complete your goals. It is one thing when you have other people doubt you, but when you start doing it, you start questioning if you really can. Well, suppose you really are passionate about what you want to do. In that case, you will begin to work against those doubtful thoughts and prove to everyone, including yourself, that you can do it.

May 17th

"Failure is the foundation of success, and the means by which it is achieved."

- Lao Tzu: Ancient Chinese Philosopher

It is bound to happen at some point; you will fail at something in college. Hopefully, you do not fail, but there will be a day when you just do not produce your best work. This is not a good time when you realize you failed something in your class. Now you wonder if you are good enough to be in this class or if you should drop it. This attitude is one of defeat. You failed one time, and you will let a single situation define this class. Instead, look at this as an opportunity to realize that you need to put in extra work in this class, and use that setback as motivation to do better in the future. Instead of looking at it as you do not know anything, look at it as a way for you to narrow down what you do know. So, you missed most of the problems on the quiz, but you used the right formulas, just in the wrong equations. So, you are narrowing down your knowledge. Pretty soon, if you continue to work at it, you will pass the next quiz, and you will realize that failure was just extra motivation to do better.

May 18th

"Life itself is the most wonderful fairy tale."
- Hans Christian Anderson: 19th Century Danish Writer

About the time of midterms, you are really not enjoying life. You study all night just to wake up and study some more. You are overwhelmed and tired and stressed out. If anyone told you to feel lucky doing what you are doing, you might punch them in the face. It is easy to get caught up in the problems you have going on right now, but it is not so bad in the long run. You will look back a few years from now and realize it was not that bad, and weirdly, it was kind of fun. Midterms are not fun, but studying with your friends is pretty fun. You live a great life, and if you cannot see it now, you will eventually. You only see the bad in your life right now. If you stop looking at only the bad, you will notice that your life is mostly good. Your life does not have to feel like a fairy tale; however, your life is pretty cool. You get to experience both the great highs and the bad lows; this is what makes life an interesting story. Do not get so down on your life, but rather be thankful that you get to have it.

May 19th

"When I walk along with two others, from at least one I will be able to learn."

- *Confucius: Ancient Chinese Philosopher*

Sometimes it is easy to write someone off as unknowledgeable based on their appearance. Some people may not appear or act like they know anything, but they probably know something you do not. Just because they are not your ideal image of a wise person, they probably have some bits of information that would benefit you. Likely, this information is not even something to do with school. As you begin your adult life, you will be more thankful for these pieces of advice on life. The best advice you may ever receive will not be about school or completing college. These bits of advice are about life. People who can give you life advice are the people you should listen to the most. This is because they have probably lived through the exact situation they are giving you advice about. These people may not always appear to have the vastest array of knowledge, but trust me, they can offer you some solid pieces of advice. All you have to do is be willing to listen to them.

May 20th

"A man without self-control is like a city broken into and left without walls."

- Proverbs 25:28

You will not fare very well in life if you do not have self-control. That is a skill that everyone learns eventually, some after a much harder and longer path. This is one of those things that the quicker you can learn and master self-control, the better you will be. People will constantly try to push your buttons, and you have to not get thrown by them doing that. There will be days where everything that can go wrong will go wrong. When you have days like this, having control of your emotions is key. You do not want to make the day worse because of your lack of emotional control. These times in your life are when the best thing you can do is control yourself and not react. Sure, you can get by with having no self-control for a little bit, but eventually, it will catch up with you, and it will not be good when it does. There is a certain amount of maturity that goes into having self-control. Maturing is knowing that you have to have more control over your emotions and actions. You will greatly benefit from controlling yourself and not letting outside events and people get under your skin.

May 21st

"Practice yourself, for heaven's sake in little things, then proceed to greater."

- Epictetus: Ancient Greek Philosopher

If you want success, you need to start doing the little things well. If you're going to succeed in your classes, you cannot overlook the small stuff. Get really good at studying, and succeed in your classes. Get really good at making a habit of going to office hours and talking to your professors, and you will see you do much better in those classes. Doing the small things are not always the most fun. Studying is often pretty boring, but you will see success in your grades if you learn how to study well. If you want to start getting good at athletics, you will have to find a skill in your sport that sets you apart from everyone else. It might be playing defense, it might be shooting, or even just out-hustling everyone. You might be surprised how much recognition you get for doing the small things well. It might not always be the most glamorous job you are doing, but it will set you apart from everyone else if you do it well. Once you master the basics, it allows you to move on up to bigger tasks. Because you got good at the small things, it makes moving up even easier.

May 22nd

"Nothing can stop the man with the right mental attitude from achieving his goal; nothing on earth can help the man with the wrong mental attitude."

- Thomas Jefferson: 3rd President of the United States

◆

We all have bitten off more than we can chew before. This means that we end up with more responsibility than what we are capable of carrying. In college, you are going to feel this from time to time. You might have three exams and a paper as well as a club meeting all in one week. In these types of situations, it is not the amount of work that will make or break you, but your attitude toward it. In this situation, you have two choices you can make: one is you think to yourself how you cannot accomplish all of this and let the situation get the better of you. The other option is that you have some optimism toward all that you need to get done, and you find some determination inside of you to get it all completed. You might have a lot that you have to accomplish, but whether you get it done or not depends on your attitude toward the issue. If you are optimistic and determined, then there really is no limit of what you can accomplish.

May 23rd

"Most powerful is he who has himself in his own power."

- *Lucius Annaeus Seneca: Roman Stoic Philosopher*

College is a time of figuring out who you are. Most likely, this is the first time you have been on your own. You have huge freedoms of choosing what you want to study and what discipline you want to major in. You also have smaller privileges like deciding where you want to eat every day or how you treat people. Some people are going to treat you poorly. There are infinite times when someone will make you angry, jealous, sad, disgusted, and so many other feelings. There are not many times when it is appropriate to show these emotions. A person who has control of their emotions has the greatest power. Having the ability to control your emotions is a critical skill to learn in college. Whether that means not exploding in anger with someone and causing a scene or having control over the nervous thoughts right before your final exams. Obviously, this is easier said than done and will require some work. However, once you manage to control yourself, you will have more power than you ever thought you had.

May 24th

"Pearls don't lie on the seashore. If you want one, you must dive for it."

- Chinese Proverb

◆

Most good things are not just lying somewhere waiting for you to find them - you are going to have to work for them. There are very few things in life that are good and require little work. It is not worth it to take that chance, so it is recommended that you just start working for it. Maybe you want to go to college and graduate, or perhaps your goal is to start making as much money as you can as soon as you can. You can also have personal goals such as getting into a loving relationship or gaining good close friends. All of these things require work. There are not just going to be people waiting around for you to find them; you will have to look and work at building a relationship with these people to gain them as a friend or a romantic partner. If you want to make money, you will have to work. Obviously working is going to require some dedication and determination. Getting a college degree will require the same perseverance and determination. There is no point in waiting around for good things to magically happen to you; you are going to have to work for them.

May 25th

"Life is not a problem to be solved, but a reality to be experienced."

- *Soren Kierkegaard: 18th century Danish Philosopher*

You might have wondered what it means to have a good life. One interpretation is that a good life is to experience everything that you can as a human. This does not mean that you should seek out only pleasures and happiness. It actually means that you should share everything—pain, hope, failure, success, happiness, sadness. If you never experience bad, you will not understand good and vice versa. Hopefully, all of you get to experience the ultimate highs of happiness, love, and success. To fully understand and appreciate these moments, you will also have to experience loss, hatred, and failure. It makes you a more complete person when you experience lots of things. Have you ever talked to someone you found interesting, and all they have experienced in life was good? Probably not. They are interesting because they have had successes in life and have also experienced the bad of life and persevered through it. Experience the good and the bad, and when you look back, you can say that you lived a full life.

May 26th

"I have not failed 10,000 times - I've successfully found 10,000 ways that will not work."

- Thomas Edison 19th Century American Inventor

Failures are inevitably going to happen to you. No person is perfect and makes the correct choices every time. There will be times when you will fail, and that is okay. Failing is often one of the first steps to succeeding. However, that does not make failing feel any better. You will forget about some schoolwork. You will fail at some relationships. Yes, they all suck right now, but as you move on, you will learn your lesson from each failure and use it as knowledge going forward. When you are down, you have to fight to get back up. The strongest person is not the one who avoids failing. It is the one who fails but can get back up and keep going each and every time. No one likes to fail because failing is not fun. Failing and giving up should not be an option for you. It might be easy to give up, but that is not the person you are. You are not a quitter. The best thing to do when you mess up is to learn from it and keep going.

May 27th

"Do every act of your life as though it were the very last act of your life."

- *Marcus Aurelius: Roman Emperor & Stoic Philosopher*

When you are going through college, you will know what it is like to not be motivated. There will be days when you do not do your best on schoolwork because you are completely unmotivated to do so. We are all human; it happens sometimes. Is that really how you want to go about everything in your life though? Think about if this was the last assignment you ever handed in; would you be happy with a C+ grade? Would you be satisfied with a half-done paper or presentation? It is hard to do something when you are not motivated. Find your own motivation to get you going and really focus on showing your best work, not just good enough work to get by. You will also be happier if you give more effort and end with a better score than a bad score for a half-effort attempt. You will be much happier if your last assignment was an A instead of a C. We are not guaranteed every day, so take time to get the right mindset to produce your best work in whatever you have to do. You will be much happier with the results when you do.

May 28th

"The great danger for most of us lies not in setting our aim to high and falling short; but in setting our aim to low, and achieving our mark."

- Michelangelo: 16th Century Italian Sculptor & Painter

Some of you have very high expectations for yourself. You might really want to be the best student in your classes. The higher you set your goals, the harder it is to not worry about falling short of those goals. Sometimes we live and do stuff, trying not to fail, rather than succeed. You will learn that sometimes to be the best student, you need to fail at a few things to really understand some of the material. Luckily for those of you who have high expectations of yourself, you can always remember that the higher your successes, the higher your failures. Sure, maybe you want to be a straight-A student, and you just scored an 85 percent on your last test. This is unacceptable, and you feel bad because of your high expectations and putting in a lot of time and effort in preparing for this test. You scored the best of anyone in the class. Sure, you failed in your expectations, but to everyone else, you succeeded. Set your goals high, so your failures surpass those around you.

May 29th

"There is nothing impossible to he who will try."'
- *Alexander The Great: Ancient Greek King*

You are lying on your bed wondering if the tasks you have taken on are going to be possible to accomplish. For some, this may look like changing your major and starting classes over again. For others, it could look like trying to make ends meet and still have enough to pay for tuition. Whatever the daunting task is in front of you, the word impossible will creep into your mind. You might think it is impossible to make ends meet, or that it will be impossible to change your major and graduate on time. The reason that your issue seems impossible to overcome is because you have not started to fix it. When you start making a plan and working on a way to figure out how to solve this challenge, you have at least given yourself a shot at accomplishing it. Convince yourself that you have a chance of making something possible, and you just might be able to do it. There will be times when you do not conquer the challenge, but trying to conquer it at least gives you the possibility of turning the impossible into possible.

May 30th

"You will not be punished for your anger; you will be punished by your anger."

- Buddha: Ancient Indian Religious Leader

It is not a problem to be angry. It is a basic human emotion that we all feel. The feeling of anger will never get you into trouble but acting out your anger will. When we become angry, we lose the ability to think clearly and rationally. Anger is a primitive emotion that turns us back into primitive creatures. How often have you done or said something that you regretted when you were angry? We have all done or said something that we wish we would not have in a moment of anger. Looking back, you realize it was dumb, but because your mind was clouded by anger, you did not consider if it was smart. This is the problem that anger causes. When angry, you are more likely to do something you will regret. It is always best to walk away from a situation and clear your head before taking action. A clear mind allows for rational thoughts, and the best decision will be made. Your best choices in life are made with a clear head and logical thinking. If you are in a situation and can feel yourself getting angry, you should clear out before you do or say something that will get you in trouble.

May 31st

"Freedom is the power to choose your own chains."
- Jean Jacques Rousseau: 18th Century Genevan Philosopher

Your newfound freedom is going to be pretty awesome. You will remember that feeling of deciding what you get to do with almost every single decision. One of the biggest freedoms you will come to realize is your time. No longer are you stuck in a building for eight hours a day. You have a few hours of class every day and the rest of the day is yours to do whatever you want. Remember that this new freedom comes with consequences. If you choose to use your free time to do nothing but go out, your school life will suffer. Likewise, if you do nothing but study, your social life will suffer. You have to find a balance of time where you can do both without letting the other one deteriorate. With your freedom of choice will come new obligations. If you join a club, you will have to spend time going to meetings and doing activities. The same can be said for Greek life, academic clubs, intermural sports, and others. What you choose to do will lead to new obligations you have to fulfill. Choose wisely what you decide to fill your newfound time with.

June

June 1st

"Difficulties strengthen the mind, as labor does the body."

- Lucius Annaeus Seneca: Roman Stoic Philosopher

Working out is a great way to strengthen the body, whether it is lifting weights or playing a sport. Physical exercise is a great way to keep the body working well. You also need to make sure you are working out the mind. Your mind is what is going to get you through college. Just like you are not always motivated to exercise your body, you will not always feel motivated to exercise your mind. Those homework assignments and chapters that you need to read are exercises for your mind. There are days when you do not feel like reading or studying. You have to push through that and find some sort of motivation. The trials and failures will make you stronger. Just as when you can finally see the progress being made from working out, you will see the mental progress you complete from working out your mind. You will become smarter in the classroom and wiser in your everyday life. Just as an unhealthy body can be harmful, so can an unhealthy mind.

June 2nd

"A man who has committed a mistake and doesn't correct it, is committing another mistake."

- Confucius: Ancient Chinese Philosopher

We all make mistakes. This should not be a huge surprise since we are all human. Being human means making mistakes. Errors often have a bad stigma around them. People believe that mistakes are bad. Mistakes themselves are not bad; the consequences are. Mistakes show us where we need to improve in life. They let us know that we are not doing something the way it should be done and we should change it going forward. See, that does not sound bad, does it? The consequences are another thing; those are tough. The shining light on it is that the effects make sure that we remember the pain so as not to make that mistake in the future. Sometimes we make a mistake and do not learn from it. If you are not going to learn from it, you will never get past this one little obstacle. If you do not understand anything from it, that is just another mistake. Learn from your mistakes, accept the consequences, and move on so you do not make the same mistake in the future.

June 3rd

"Anything or anyone capable of angering you becomes your master."

- Epictetus: Ancient Greek Philosopher

One of the most infuriating times in college is when you sit at a desk looking at a problem on a homework assignment or even a test. You have been trying to figure out this problem for what feels like hours, and you just have no idea how to tackle it. You start to feel some annoyance and frustration bubble up inside of you. You might say to yourself, "Why can I not figure this stupid problem out?" This problem has now taken hold of your feelings and can now control them. This one problem will make you lose your cool because you cannot figure out how to solve it? You should not let something like this get you upset. Sure, it is frustrating now, but take a break and return to it. When you come back, you will have composed yourself enough to think clearly. When you do this, you give yourself a clear mind, which often allows you to figure out the problem. Do not be controlled by something other than yourself. Figure out what you need to change about yourself or the situation to control anger.

June 4th

"If you want a rainbow, you have to deal with the rain."

- Augustus: First Roman Emperor

You know that there cannot be good without bad. Sometimes we deal with a rainbow; other times, we deal with the rain. There is good news for both of these situations. If life is like a rainbow right now, then enjoy it and everything that the good has to offer. You are reaping the benefits of your work, and everyone deserves at least a little time to enjoy their accomplishments. This also means that you cannot get too used to this good because there is always some bad out there. So, enjoy the good, but do not expect it to stay like this forever. You know what a rainstorm is like. Rainstorms do not last forever, just like the bad in your life. Sure, it is dark and gloomy now, but pretty soon, the rain will pass, and what will be left is good. Have faith that you will get through this hard time in your life. You can also keep your spirits up by knowing that as soon as this bad storm in your life passes, there will be a nice rainbow to greet you. You are going to have some sunny days and some stormy days. You will have some bad days, but that means that a good day is coming soon.

June 5th

"The only person you are destined to become is the person you decide to be."

- Ralph Waldo Emerson: 19th Century American Philosopher

What do you want to be when you grow up? This is the question you were asked all throughout your childhood. Now that you are in college, you have the opportunity to become whatever you want. What you decide on becoming is who you will be. No one is pushing you to do the right thing or to make sure you take care of yourself as much anymore. You need to push yourself with a goal in mind to become what you want to be. If you decide you no longer want to go to class and blow off all of your obligations, then you are destined for failure. If you decide on going to class and creating a schedule to attend to all your obligations, then you have destined yourself for something better. It becomes much easier to neglect your schoolwork and responsibilities when you do not have parents and teachers watching over you. This is why it is important to get disciplined and really stick with it. Practice what you want to become, and you will become what you practiced. The more disciplined you are, and the more you practice it, the better your destiny will be.

June 6th

"Settle on the type of person you want to be and stick to it, whether alone or in company."

- Marcus Aurelius: Roman Emperor & Stoic Philosopher

It is easy to do something when everyone around you is supportive of you or does it as well. Once you go off to college, you realize that you can choose to reinvent yourself and become a completely new person. Look at what you want to be and what you want to do, and settle on becoming that. If you want to be a doctor, you can be if you put the work in. Once you decide on your goal, you need to stick to that plan and work every day to obtain that goal. The problem is there will be people around you who do not want to support you reaching that goal. They will entice you to do things that prevent you from your ultimate goal. It will take a bit of mental toughness and determination to do this. You might lose some friends along the way, but if they did not want to help you succeed, were they really your friends to begin with? Many people have walked a thousand miles in your shoes. It is your turn to take that walk.

June 7th

"Brave men rejoice in adversity, just as brave soldiers triumph in war."

- Lucius Annaeus Seneca: Roman Stoic Philosopher

♦

If you want to have success in your classes, you have to accept a couple of failures without getting down on yourself. There will be times when you show up to class and do all the assignments, and when it comes time for a quiz, you bomb it. It is pretty easy to be discouraged when you feel you are trying your best and still fail. What you will learn in these moments is that failure is just a lesson and something to build off of toward success. Yes, you will miss a few tests answers, but you will be glad that you did in the long run. The reason for this is because it shows you what you need to focus on learning and pushes you to try even harder. During these times of failure, it is easier to lose motivation than to keep trying your hardest. You have to walk away from these failures with some delight because now you know what you need to work on specifically. If you can stay positive during those trying times, it will help you get to the successful times when you can really enjoy it.

June 8th

"How much time one saves who does not look to see what their neighbor says or does or thinks."

- Marcus Aurelius: Roman Emperor & Stoic Philosopher

One of the biggest lessons you learn is to focus on yourself. If you worry about what others think about you, you will live a very anxious life. If you stopped spending so much time worrying about what others think of you or what they are doing without you, you would have so much more time and so much less anxiety. This can be hard if you are a people pleaser. You might have always struggled worrying about if other people liked you or not. This can lead to a lot of stress and worry and probably annoyed everyone around you because of your fear. It is tough to stop this habit, but it can be done. If you can remind yourself to stop worrying about what someone thinks and just do what needs to be done, eventually, you just start to do it without thinking about it. You are not going to impress everyone. There will be people who just do not like you for no reason. If you can accept this and cut yourself some slack, you will live a happier, better life.

June 9th

"It is during our darkest moments that we must focus on the light."

- Aristotle: Ancient Greek Philosopher

You will have some bad days in college. Now, what you consider a bad day is different from person to person. During these bad times, it is important to focus on something good to get you through the bad. What you have to realize is that the light will shine eventually. While it is pretty dark now, that does not mean it always will be. If you can focus on something that passes the time a little easier, that is what you need to do. Maybe you will go out this weekend with some friends, which gives you something to get you through the week. Maybe watching a comedy in your room at night is enough to get you through the day. These tough times in college can really be a struggle if you do not know how to properly handle them. You can go into a really low place if you do not have some light at the end of the tunnel to help you make it. Find what makes you happy, and use it to help you. You cannot avoid these bad times, but what you can do is find the things that bring you joy to get you through those bad times.

June 10th

"In the end, it's not the years in your life that count. It's the life in your years."

- Abraham Lincoln: 16th President of the United States

Are you going to college to get an education? Yes. Is getting an education the only thing you need to worry about? Absolutely not. You are finally in college; you deserve to have some fun. College is also pretty stressful at times, so if you do not have fun, you will be one miserable person. Make these years worth it, and fill them with memories and good times. This does not mean skip class and party all the time. You can make the most out of your college by truly enjoying your college classes. That does not mean you just go to class and get through it, but rather that you make friends and engage in the class. You can make college classes enjoyable and mix that with some well-deserved partying and fun with friends. Then you will have some seriously great memories. It will be good for you to see that you did both the hard work of college and rewarded yourself with the fun that comes with the college atmosphere. Do not look back on college as only partying or only classes. Try to make the most of both of them.

June 11th

"Love only what falls your way and is fated for you. What could suit you more than that?"

- Marcus Aurelius: Roman Emperor & Stoic Philosopher

It stinks looking around and seeing everyone around you happy in a relationship while you are single, doesn't it? Even your ex has found someone mere days after ending it with you. A four-year relationship ended, and they are on ice cream dates with someone else. Sometimes it feels like you just are not meant to be with anyone. You might feel like you should not go out and look for someone because it just is not worth it. The good news is that you will eventually find someone. If they are the right person, you will find each other. Fate has a weird way of giving us something, even when we least expect it. Maybe instead of actively trying to talk to someone that is not fully interested in you, you move on and start looking for someone who will be. If they are genuinely interested in you, they will take the time to talk. Go out and let fate guide you to the person who was meant to be with you. What better way to fall in love than that?

June 12th

"Don't be pushed by your problems; be led by your dreams."

- Ralph Waldo Emerson: 19th Century American Philosopher

We are often pushed in a direction for the wrong reasons. We usually go in to avoid our problems, even if we have to give up on some of our dreams. This is the completely wrong route to go. You should not be driven by your problems; you should be driven by your dreams. The path to your goals will be riddled with issues and problems. Problems are a part of life; they are necessary to have success. Sure, they are not fun to go through, but afterward, you are a stronger and better person because of them. When you come across a problem in your life, rather than letting that problem control where you will go, you should dictate the problem. By this, you should figure out a way to handle the problem and use that strategy to get through it. If you are constantly running and avoiding problems, you will be totally exhausted. It is usually easier to deal with a problem than to continually run from it in the grand scheme. The direction you should go in life is the way of your dreams and ambition; do not let a few problems throw you off course.

June 13th

"The most difficult thing is the decision to act. The rest is merely tenacity."

- Amelia Earhart: 20th Century Aviator

As with most decisions, you choose to act upon the situation or do nothing. There are times when doing nothing is your best option, but this page is not about that. You have been checking out that cute girl or guy in your class who you see every day. You obviously are into them, but you are way too nervous about approaching them. Well, this is one of those times when you have the choice to act or not. What is holding you back? The worst thing that happens is that they tell you no. If the answer is no, you move on and find someone else. But imagine if you never go over and talk to them. The hardest part is convincing yourself to go over and talk to them. Once you convince yourself to go, everything else is just keeping up the courage to not give up on your walk over. Some of the best things in life require convincing yourself to act on the situation. Who knows what special things are in your future if you do?

June 14th

"It is better to fail in originality than to succeed in imitation."

- Herman Melville: 19th Century American Novelist

◆

We are all trying to impress someone. It can be professors, peers, or someone you are romantically chasing. In each of these cases, we want to show off who we are, but by doing this, we often lose sight of who we really are as individuals. It is important that while impressing others, you stay true to yourself. It can be hard to be yourself in a situation where you know being like someone else works better. It can be pretty easy in college to copy a paper that someone wrote and get a good score on it, but that is not staying true to yourself. You have the ability to write your own unique paper that gets a good score. You do not have to act like someone else to get others to like you. Sometimes, people will just not like you, and that is okay. You do not have to be liked by everyone in your frat or always get the highest scores in class. By being unique and your own person, you will find a way to get good scores in class, and you will find the people who appreciate you for who you are. Why would you want to live the life of someone else, when you are already unique yourself?

June 15th

"Knowing yourself is the beginning of all wisdom."
- *Aristotle: Ancient Greek Philosopher*

You obviously know that you will learn a thing or two while at college, at least, hopefully you do. You will relearn some things that you probably have some general knowledge of. Like when taking a biology course, you can think back to your high school biology class and use some of the same principles that you learned then. However, you are going to learn a bunch of stuff that you had no idea you would ever know. Your mind will be opened to so many different ideas, both in the classroom and outside of it. You will learn a bunch of new subjects and ideas in college. If you look at your course catalog, it will hit you that your university offers courses on topics you have never heard of before. You are also going to learn some new life lessons. There have been several times when you will leave a situation and think to yourself, Wow, I never thought I would have learned that. You will learn new things about yourself that you never thought you would know. You will start liking new people, places, music, etc. This is a wonderful time to find out so much about yourself and the world around you.

June 16th

"I attribute my success to this: I never gave or took any excuses."

- Florence Nightingale: 19th Century English Statistician

You can go out on a limb and say that everyone wants to be successful in college and life. Very rarely do you see someone want to fail at college or life. There are several ways to obtain success, and one of the biggest is eliminating excuses. Everyone has something bad that has happened to them, but that does not mean that it gives you the right to not do something because of it. If you can get rid of excuses in your life and excuses from others, you will find yourself on the path to success. If you keep giving excuses for why you did not get your assignments completed, you will not have success in the classroom. If your friend keeps giving excuses as to why they have not seen you in years, you are not having success in your relationships. No matter where you look, you can find an opportunity for you or someone around you to give an excuse. If you constantly use and even accept excuses, you will never make headway to success. Try to eliminate excuses out of your life; this is a great stepping-stone to a successful life.

June 17th

"You cannot dream yourself into a character; you must hammer and forge yourself one."

- James Anthony Froude: 19th Century English Historian & Novelist

---

Often, you will hop on social media and see what other people are up to. You see other people traveling and doing some fun things. You read the caption as they attempt to tell you what all they are doing in life. These captions and pictures do not do justice to what life is really like. Do not look to social media to see what life is about. If you want to know what that party was like, go out and party. If you want to know what that city offers, go travel and visit it. You can do all of these things and never say one word on social media. This is not to say that you should never post on social media. You have to go out and experience life. You do not want to look back and wish that you would have gone out to experience all these wonderful places and events. No post can bring light to something the same way that seeing it in person can.

June 18th

"Life is never fair, and perhaps it is a good thing for most of us that it is not."

- Oscar Wilde: 19th Century Irish Poet

◆

There will be times when you tell yourself that life is not fair. Your longtime partner just broke up with you seemingly out of nowhere. They go and run to someone else and date them right after they left you. They talk badly about you to their friends, and you are left in the dust wondering, what did I do to deserve this? Life's unfairness is sometimes a blessing in disguise. You are alone and have some time to reflect on who you are as a person. Now that you are single, you can really take inventory of what you offer and give to another person. You are probably hurt and angry at the decision of this other person. You now want to go out and prove to everyone that you do not need anyone to succeed. This drive and newfound passion for success and life is an unseen product of the unfair acts you have endured. So yes, there are times when life is not fair, and these are the times when you are going to have a new excitement in life and a new drive for something better.

June 19th

"There is only one way to avoid criticism: do nothing, say nothing, and be nothing."

- Aristotle: Ancient Greek Philosopher

Most people do not like being criticized. Whether it is meant to be or not, we often take these critiques to heart. Most of the time, these criticisms are not intended to be hurtful; it is just how other people disagree on how you could do something better. You might think that you just will not do anything that people can critique. Good luck finding something that people will not critique. The other thing is that literally almost every great thing you see today was critiqued at some point. Beautiful works of art were critiqued at one point. Even modern scientific discoveries that help humanity were not seen as revolutionary at the time. If you do not want to be critiqued, you will contribute nothing to society. Not everything you do or say is going to be everyone's favorite, and that is okay. You have to do it because it is what you want and something you think will benefit the greater good.

June 20th

"The darker the night, the brighter the stars; the deeper the grief, the closer is God!"

- Apollon Maykov: 19th Century Russian Poet

It is unfortunate that some of the greatest years of your life can take a quick turn for the worst. You may receive news that a family member has passed away or been diagnosed with cancer or you may have a sudden end to a longtime relationship. Not only do you have to deal with the grief and suffering of these events, but you also must continue to uphold your responsibilities of being a college student. This can be a tough act to juggle. It is during these moments that you have to find the light in those dark moments. You may have lost a loved one, but they are now in a better place, and the bonds you have created with those around you have been strengthened through by the loss. Grief allows you to see what is really important in life. You no longer value material goods; you now wish good health for your sick relatives or peace for those struggling with the loss of someone from their life. Grief is not easy to overcome, but if you can remain optimistic that the hurt will ease, you will have peace.

June 21st

"Fate leads the willing and drags the reluctant."
- Lucius Annaeus Seneca: Roman Stoic Philosopher

Whether you believe in fate or not, you can think of it as your individual decision. These decisions that you make always lead you closer or further from what you want. If you want your fate to lead you to graduate from college, then your decision to study or not is a choice that will either get you one step closer to your destiny or have no progress. If you are willing to make the decisions that will best project you toward your ultimate goals, you are leading your own destiny. It is in your hands, and you are taking full control of fate. Like most things in life, it is better to take control of something while you can. If you have the option to choose, why would you not? Not taking control and being forced is not something anyone really likes to do. You will either get to your fate by your own doing, or it will inevitably make its way to you, albeit less favorable than if you took control.

June 22nd

"Each of us lives only now, this brief instant. The rest has been lived already, or is impossible to see."

- Marcus Aurelius: Roman Emperor & Stoic Philosopher

It is part of the learning process to make mistakes. You just have to learn to forgive yourself for them and move on. We have all made mistakes in our past, and unfortunately, we cannot go back and rewrite history. That gut feeling of not changing something or wishing you would have done something different really hurts. It is hard to move on from those feelings. Still, if you can live each day and remind yourself that you are human and will make mistakes, you will hopefully soon be able to forgive yourself. The past cannot be changed; the same can be said for the future. The future is already out there and cannot be changed yet. It is impossible to know totally what is yet to come. So really, the only time period that you have absolute power of is now. Accept the past as unchangeable and the future as unpredictable, and enjoy this current moment. Do what you need to do to make up for the past and improve the end.

June 23rd

"As fire tests gold, so misfortune tests brave men."
- Lucius Annaeus Seneca: Roman Stoic Philosopher

Is everything crumbling in your life? Maybe you just failed a test, your car will not start, and then your roommate starts arguing with you. It kind of feels like nothing in your life can go right. These misfortunes allow us to grow to be stronger and better people. It is about the mindset you have with these misfortunes. These misfortunes will mold you into a stronger individual, as weird as it sounds. Instead of feeling like failure when you failed your test, rather see it as a learning opportunity, and that was your sign that you needed to grow in that subject. How are you supposed to know what you enjoy without failing at a few things? When we first started to walk, we did not give up the first time we fell down. Imagine what would have happened if we said, "I do not know how to walk; I quit." It is humanly impossible to be great at everything we try. If everyone was great at everything, then there would be nothing that makes us unique. It is okay to be disappointed when you fail, but do not think of yourself as a failure; rather, it is an opportunity to grow.

June 24th

"Courage is not having the strength to go on; it is going on when you don't have the strength."

- Theodore Roosevelt: 26th President of the United States

There are times when you sit down and start to question if the path you are on is too hard and if you should just stop now. If you stop now, you could have a decent life and would not have to keep working as hard. This is very enticing to people, especially those with high goals that take a while to complete. You are tired, and it is easy to stop and just accept the easier life for now. This is not the way to live. You should never settle for less than what you are capable of. This goes for everything in your life. You should never give less effort than you are capable of. The only way you will complete your dreams is if you give maximum effort at all times. Think of the life that you want. The reason it is so amazing is that you have set the bar so high. You have to keep climbing to get to that life. Do not settle for this mediocre life you want to stop for now. This was not your goal, and you will be disappointed someday if you do not keep going.

June 25th

"When in Rome, do as the Romans."
- English Proverb

It can be pretty scary when you set foot on campus as a freshman. You have pretty much no idea what you are doing or even where you are going. You really do not know how this whole college thing works. You will soon learn that balancing social life and studying can be a pretty thin line to walk. What should you do to learn how to be more successful in college? Well, you find someone who has been in college for a couple of years and knows what they are doing. One of the best things you can ever do is become friends with some classmates who happen to be a few years older than you. They can give you advice on balancing school and a life outside of the classroom. They may even help introduce you to some new friends. It is never wrong to look up to someone older. They can help you get accustomed to this new world that you are in. College is unfamiliar territory for many new students. Find someone who knows what they are doing, and watch what they do. This can really help you learn the ropes and get a good start to your college career.

June 26th

"Nothing can bring you peace but yourself."
- Ralph Waldo Emerson: 19th Century American Philosopher

You are going to meet so many new people at this point in your life. You are also going to have times when you are alone. Do you enjoy being alone with yourself? This question will affect many areas of your life. You are going to have to start to become pretty cool being with yourself. This can be hard if you have always been around friends and family your whole life. This can also become a problem if have been in a long-term relationship since high school. You have never had the opportunity to be alone with yourself, and when you find yourself with no one around, how will you be? Usually, many people have some inner demons they have not figured out how to get rid of because they have never had a day alone with themselves to figure that out. The sooner you can get comfortable with yourself, the better off you will be. When you have times when you are completely alone, it will not be a difficult and hard time; you might actually find some peace with it. Become friends with yourself, and you will benefit in all aspects of your life.

June 27th

"Before anything else, preparation is the key to success."
- Alexander Graham Bell: 18th Century Scottish Inventor

The key to getting good grades in your college classes is going to class and doing well on the exams. It sounds easier than it really is. Unless you are one of the few really gifted people who do not study, barely go to class, and still do amazingly, that is not how you will succeed. What the majority of us have to do is prepare for our courses. This means doing the work outside of class in preparation for the next class. You will have to study for the tests and read to understand the next class's lectures. Because for the majority of us, if we do not properly prepare, we will fail badly. Sometimes it sucks having to sit at your desk and read countless pages, but it will pay off for your future in that class. Because now that you understand the textbook, you will use that knowledge to help you understand the lectures. Now that you know the book and the courses, you will have a good base to do well on the exams. Preparing for each of your classes is the key to having success.

June 28th

"Pleasure becomes punishment when taken beyond a certain point."

- Epictetus: Ancient Greek Philosopher

Like with most things, you have to experiment to know the limits of what you can do. With that being said, we all know that too much fun can typically lead to some pretty bad consequences. A great example is food. Eating out every once in awhile will never hurt, but the more you eat out, the worse you are going to feel. Fast food is enjoyable, but too much fast food can lead to a pretty drastic increase in weight. The same goes for most things. Think of anything that brings you happiness, and if done too much, it usually has some bad consequences. There is never anything wrong with doing things that bring you pleasure, as long as you can moderate it. Remember, the limits on which the satisfaction you feel will outweigh the effects. If you start wondering if the consequences outweigh the pleasure, it is probably time to stop. As long as you are smart enough to know when to stop, you can have the most fun possible, and who does not want that?

June 29th

"It is not the length of life, but depth of life."
- *Ralph Waldo Emerson: 19th Century American Philosopher*

If someone asks what you love about the life you live right now, how would you answer? Do you want to start getting academic accolades, or do you want to meet new people? Think about what kind of life you want to live, and then go out and live it. You are totally free to finally make that decision. The only thing you have to do is make sure you love the life you are living. You should go to bed every night thinking, "I love my life." You know you have a good life when you can do that. Make those friends and start winning those awards if you want that out of your life. No matter what it is that you want, just make sure that you love the process. It is easy to love life when constantly succeeding at it. When you get nothing, you should still smile and think about how awesome of a life you live. That is another sign of a good life. Even when things are not going your way, you are still happy with the life that you are living. If you can say that about your life, good or bad, then you are living pretty well.

June 30th

"For the things we have to learn before we can do them, we learn by doing them."

- Aristotle: Ancient Greek Philosopher

Many of you have learned to play an instrument. Like many things in life, you probably did not pick up this instrument and play it well the first time. It probably took some time even getting a decent sound to come out of it. You then learned some notes and practiced those notes. You got better and started learning more and more notes until you could begin to play music. From there, it became easier to pick up more difficult pieces of music. All of that practice and gradual steps allowed you to do well at playing that instrument. You can use that format for almost anything in life that you want to be good at. The first time you pick it up, you might not be so good. The key to getting good is practicing. Just as you practiced different notes and music, you have to practice the small things to get good at something. If you are willing to put the work in with practice, you will start to see results. Getting good at something is not always a quick path, so do not be discouraged if you are not great at something the first time. With a bit of practice and some time, you soon will be.

July

July 1st

"It's not what happens to you, but how you react to it that matters."

- Epictetus: Ancient Greek Philosopher

Many trials will arise in your life through college. Not only will these trials come from your education, but from life as well. There are countless examples of this. Maybe you got a bad score on a test you absolutely had to do good on. Or perhaps someone unexpectedly leaves your life. Whatever it is, these problems suck. There is no nice way to say it, but we cannot let these problems completely incapacitate us from continuing on with our lives. Sure, it is hard to know what to do after something bad happens. No one can blame you for this feeling of uncertainty. This uncertainty is the fork in the road of your life. You now have some options to choose from. You can either bounce back and become stronger from this problem or continue to feel bad. It is never wrong to take some time to let the emotions settle, and maybe sadness is one of them. But you cannot be sad about something all of your life; it will prohibit you from living life to its fullest. When you come to that fork in the road, take the road to make a bigger comeback, and you will be surprised at the good that will come from it.

July 2nd

"Peace is liberty in tranquility."
- Marcus Tullius Cicero: Roman Statesman & Philosopher

You are in college now, and you have more freedoms than you have ever had. You at least need to have some common sense, so you are not abusing this newly possessed freedom. Just because you have some self-control does not mean that everyone you know will. You might feel a certain amount of responsibility to take care of your friends. You are going to learn that you are not going to make anyone do something they do not want. If this person wants to act without good character, you will not make them. You should also know it is not your job to take care of them; all you really need to worry about is yourself. The behaviors of your friends are their issues, not yours. You have enough to worry about when you are at college. Being the parent of another college student should not be one of them. You just need to focus on what you can control and not worry about those things outside your control. You will feel more at peace with yourself and the world if you focus on yourself and let your friends figure out how to control themselves.

July 3rd

"We can complain because rose bushes have thorns, or rejoice because thorn bushes have roses."

- Abraham Lincoln: 16th President of the United States

Things are not always going to go your way. That is okay. It spices your life up a little bit—keeps you on your toes. You will have last-minute situations pop up, and they will interfere with some plans you might already have. It is easy to start to get frustrated and even upset in these moments. You know, this was not how today was supposed to go. Instead of getting aggravated that things are not going your way, you should start thinking about how to ride this wave and turn this into a favorable situation. Was it dumb that your roommate locked themselves out of your apartment? Yes. Do you also have a test you have to get to? Of course. Can you run a key to your roommate and listen to some pump-up music to get you ready for the test? Absolutely. You can always try to turn the bad situations into something good. Rather than being upset that those situations are not working out in your favor, look for ways that you can ride out those situations to a favorable outcome.

July 4th

"We must make the best of those ills which cannot be avoided."

- Alexander Hamilton: Founding Father of the United States

It is easy to make the best out of a good situation. There is no downside to the problem, so you can enjoy every aspect of it. What do you typically do with a bad situation? Many people either avoid the bad situations or just trudge through them. It is impossible to prevent problems, just as it is impossible to prevent good conditions. Yes, you can just try to get through a bad situation, and sometimes this is the only option you have. You should try to make the best out of a bad situation if you can. The first step in making the best of a bad situation is to just accept it as it is. These situations allow us to look at any lessons we can take away from a problem. Was this situation worse because of you, and could you have done something to have this situation not happen again? If you can find any sort of answer, this is good because you can avoid this situation in the future. If you can walk out of a bad situation with a few lessons learned and no long-term major issues left, then you managed to make something good out of a pretty bad thing.

July 5th

"The best things in life are free."
- English Proverb

Going into college, you might think that the best things are a new car and the newest apartment in your college town. After a while, you will find out that the best things are the free things. You realize that groceries cost a lot of money when you pay for your groceries yourself, with your own money. You also acknowledge that clothes and shoes are expensive when you buy them. Come to think of it, everything is costly. So, when your parents are in town and offer to take you to dinner, you take them up on the offer because it is a free meal. You also should go because they are your parents, so you need to see them every once in a while. If a college club is handing out free T-shirts, go up and ask for your size. It does not matter if it is a bad-looking T-shirt because if it is, then it is one you wear to sleep in. Think of all of the money you save when you get a free T-shirt or a meal with your parents. It is a gift when you do not have to pay. So, enjoy the freebees in life, and never skip out on an opportunity for a free meal or shirt.

July 6th

"Where the way is hardest, there go thou; Follow your own path and let people talk."
- *Dante Alighieri: 13th Century Italian Poet & Writer*

The path that you are going to take in life is not going to be an easy walk. College is not going to be easy; it is going to push you mentally, maybe more than you are used to. Just because it is hard does not mean that it is the wrong path for you; it just means that you are going to have to get stronger. If the road that you are on is the one that your heart desires, then you will have no problem getting stronger to overcome these challenges. Becoming stronger does not always mean physically stronger. Sometimes it is mentally stronger; other times, it is spiritually stronger. No matter what path you take, people are going to talk about your decisions. They might not think you are strong enough to go down that path, or that it is not what they would have done. The great thing about choosing your own path in life is that it is no one's but your own. Let the people talk, and let the trials show up; you are strong enough to conquer both.

July 7th

"Gratitude is not only the greatest of virtues, but the parent of all others."

- Marcus Tullius Cicero: Roman Statesman & Philosopher

You will start to realize that there are a lot of "every man for himself" moments in college and the world. You are not given anything; it is all earned. There are also moments when things are provided to you. In both of these situations, it is always best to be gracious. You look better when you can win or lose with grace. Always be grateful for what others do for you. Most of the time, they do it just to make you happy. Never take these times for granted. People will respect you more when you show grace at your best and worst. When you can do this, you also show humility and humbleness. Think of all the other great traits that come from gratitude. You learn to show kindness and fairness when others have shown you that in the past. Respect others just as they have respect for you. You are grateful for all of these acts of kindness that others have shown you, so you do them to others. You become a better person when you can show graciousness, and the people around you also benefit from it too.

July 8th

"It is the mark of an educated mind to be able to entertain a thought without accepting it."

- Aristotle: Ancient Greek Philosopher

Too often, we throw out the opinions and thoughts of others because we do not agree with them. It is never wrong to disagree with someone; however, it is wrong to completely disregard their opinions just because you do not like their stance. This does not mean that you have to agree with every thought that a person presents to you. You can have engaging conversations with other people by entertaining a thought even if you disagree with them. This allows both parties to have a deeper, more meaningful discussion about a particular subject. Today, we are all too quick to disregard someone's thoughts just because we disagree with them. Have a conversation and listen to the reasoning behind their thoughts. You can put yourself in their shoes and understand how they may have come to the conclusions that they did. From there, you can still say you do not agree, but at least you have a better understanding of why you do not agree and where they are coming from.

July 9th

"Don't be satisfied with the stories, how things have gone with others. Unfold your own myth."

- Rumi: 13th Century Persian Poet

We all have dreams that we want to accomplish. Some of these dreams you can complete now; others you will have to wait a while. If your plan is to be a better student. You can start now by taking the appropriate steps and working toward becoming a better student. Getting your diploma is a dream that you can begin now but will require some work and perseverance to complete down the road. However, we often get lost about when we can and cannot start our dreams. We put them off, but unfortunately, these dreams will forever stay in that "later" phase. If you can create your dream now, then go out and start. Nothing says you cannot begin to move toward your goal until later in life. Go start that business on the side. It may one day take over for your current full-time job. Go start singing and painting and writing. You do not have to be middle-aged adults to start any of those. If you believe that you can complete your dreams, you can accomplish them.

July 10th

"To be even minded is the greatest virtue."
- Heraclitus: Ancient Greek Philosopher

Having an even mind will benefit you in so many different ways in college and the rest of your life. It will keep the frustration from boiling over when you cannot figure out a homework problem in college. It will keep your nerves at bay when you have to answer a question in front of the class. Even in the future it will keep you from getting overly angry with your spouse or children in life. Having an even mind will help you in crunch time during finals week or at your new job. It helps keep the bad thoughts away when you need to stay positive for everyone else's sake. Usually, nothing good comes from a situation where you reacted based on your emotions alone. Not reacting out of pure emotion can save you from both heartache and headache. It shows that you are mature and have your life together enough to not lose your cool at the slightest inconvenience. You will have a better experience with almost everything if you can be chill with how any situation plays out. There really is no downside to having an even mind.

July 11th

"The wise man accepts his pain, endures it, but does not add to it."

- Marcus Aurelius, Roman Emperor & Stoic Philosopher

Think about this: A student has a homework assignment due today, and they completely forget to do it. They decided to skip class today and finish it. They sit down to do the assignment but get distracted on their phone and decide to just put off the work until that evening. Come evening, they are too tired to do it and put it off again until tomorrow. The next day they still do not do the assignment and decide to skip class again to catch up with a friend. After about two weeks of skipping classes, they now have six missing assignments and lose credit for each class they missed. Mistakes happen; we all make them. You need to accept the error with the assignment and go to class and receive whatever consequences that follow. The worst thing you can do is compile the issue until it is too large to come back from. It is easy to make up a single assignment in college. It is much more difficult to make up half a semester's worth of work. You will make mistakes in classes; it is part of college. Make sure you do not let those mistakes accumulate into a larger problem.

July 12th

"If you are patient in one moment of anger, you will escape a hundred days of sorrow."

- Chinese Proverb

You have had a bad day in class, and you are really overwhelmed with everything you have to do. You have not eaten and are really on edge. Your roommate comes in and accidentally knocks your books and papers off the table. You get up angrily and start to rip your roommate for their slight mistake. You said a few things that you did not mean but did not think about in your fit of anger. Now your roommate has not talked to you for a few days, and you feel bad. In a few weeks, months, or even years, you both will forget why you had a bad day and even the accidental spill of your books and papers. What will not be overlooked are the mean things that you said. The words you say to others are the last thing they will forget about you. What you say to the people around you now might affect how those people think of you in five years. Talk to others with spitefulness. They will remember that. Keep your patience when you feel angry, and you will not have to worry about angry words.

July 13th

"There is more happiness in giving than receiving."

- Acts 20:35

Now that you are on your own, you will finally start making decisions for yourself. It is great that you have the freedom to make those fun new decisions that only affect you. A great thing that you can do with your recent freedom of choice is to choose to help others. This is a win-win situation for you. You get to help someone out, which will make you feel good about yourself. No one is saying you have to go out and solve the world's problems, but you can go out and help your friend move into their apartment or help someone in need. The smallest gestures of help can be very big to the person that you are helping out. There are many opportunities in and around your college campus for the sole purpose of helping others. You live a busy life, but take a few moments out of your week to help others, and leave feeling good about yourself. Enjoy the feeling of helping others out in their time of need. What better way to live than to be happy with yourself while spreading that to others?

July 14th

"Experience is simply the name we give our mistakes."
- Oscar Wilde: 19th Century Irish Poet

As you may have found out when you got to college, being an adult is not easy. You are starting to get some insight into what adult life in the "real world" is like. Life is not always going to be fair. In fact, sometimes it is just plain mean. If you want to have success in this new journey of yours, you will have to adapt and learn with each situation. Your path will not always be a straight and obvious one, nor will it be an easy trek. On your path to success, you will come across many failures and setbacks. Whether this is caused by your own doing or others, you will have to learn to overcome these problems. The mistakes, failures, and problems that you overcome will allow you to gain more insight on how to maneuver your journey. The foundation of your own success will come from the lessons and experience you acquire from those failures and setbacks. Do not think of these as bad things, but rather as a chance to learn and create a more solid foundation for your climb to your own personal success.

July 15th

"To succeed in life, you need two things: ignorance and confidence."

- Mark Twain: 19th Century American Writer

It is always good to have goals in life. It gives you purpose and meaning. Some of your goals may not always be the most straightforward and simple. This is where it is good to have a bit of ignorance and confidence. This combination can really make any goal of yours achievable. Sometimes, the odds of completing the goal are stacked up against you. You will need a bit of ignorance to ignore those statistics and just do what you believe is right. People will tell you that your plan will not work, or a statistic will say that it is highly unlikely that you make it. Being ignorant of this information can help you focus on your goal rather than what everyone says about it. You will also have to have some confidence to complete your goals. It is almost impossible to do anything if you do not have at least a tiny bit of confidence in it. Confidence is key in doing anything. So, be confident in your plan and your ability, and you will be able to complete your goal. Mix confidence and ignorance together, and you might just be unstoppable.

July 16th

"All that exists will soon change."
- Marcus Aurelius: Roman Emperor & Stoic Philosopher

So, you graduated from high school and are off to college. You have a big group of high school friends and a significant other. You had always known what you wanted to be when you grew up, and now it is finally time to begin the process. That is until you realize that you no longer like the field of study you thought you would. You also recognize that most of your friends went off to other colleges, and now your significant other randomly breaks up with you on a Wednesday night. Your whole world is crashing in, and you do not know what to do. Do not always expect everything to be the same as when you went to college. Things change as you get older. People will change; they will no longer be who you thought they were. You will change; you will have different preferences and likes as you get older and start to experience new things. Change is tough, but that does not mean that it is bad. You will find your true calling, and if it is intended to be, you will reconnect with those friends and significant others. Do not fear change. Embrace it.

July 17th

"The more man mediates upon good thought, the better will be his world and the world at large."

- Confucius: Ancient Chinese Philosopher

The more good you think about, the more interest you notice not only in you but in the world around you. You will start to see that when you feel good, the things around you begin to radiate that same good energy. When you feel good, that feeling can rub off on others and make their day better. You are not going to feel good every day. There are always going to be bad things that bring us down. When the people around you are radiating good energy, you cannot help but start to feel that energy too. If you were having a bad day, it would help make it better. You love to have your day go better, so why not bring that to others when they are down. There will always be negatives that will try to get you down. Sometimes it is just going to happen; other times, you have the choice to react either positively or negatively. It is often easy to respond negatively, but is that how you want to feel the rest of the day? Think happy and bring happy thoughts to not only yourself but those around you too.

July 18th

"Make the best use of what is in your power and take the rest as it happens."

- Epictetus: Ancient Greek Philosopher

There are plenty of things that fall outside of your control. From having people in your life who treat you poorly, to something like the library not having a book that you need. So, what do you do when these things that you cannot control happen? You could yell at the librarian for not having the book, or you could use the resources available to you to find another way to get the book. When people are treating you poorly, do you try to change them, or just walk away? There will be many situations that you encounter where you are forced to make the best out of a bad situation. When encountering a bad situation, you have to consider what you can control, and what you cannot. For those things that you can control, do something about it. Use the internet to find the book, and walk away from people who do not treat you right. For those things that you cannot control, you just have to shrug your shoulders, move on, and leave it be. You do not need to worry about what is beyond your power; control what you can, and leave the rest up to the universe.

July 19th

"The unexamined life is not worth living."
- Socrates: Ancient Greek Philosopher

What are you living for? In other words, what is your purpose in life? You have reason to always strive to live up to your potential. At least one person in your life wants to see you reach your potential. Never mind what someone else wants from you; you also have to want to get it. If all you do every day is wake up, eat some food, then go to bed, is that really all you are capable of? You should constantly evaluate yourself to see if you are doing all that you are capable of doing. You can change not only yourself but something in this world. You have goals to accomplish and dreams to chase. There is almost no end to the things you are capable of doing. If you look back on your life, are you happy with the things you have done? If you are, you are living right, so keep that up. If you are not, it is time to make up for lost time and start becoming what you were meant to be. The last thing you want forty years from now is to look back on your life and see regret and all the things you wish you could have done. Reach for your potential directly, so you never have to look back with regret.

July 20th

"They must change often, who would be constant in happiness."

- Confucius: Ancient Chinese Philosopher

Things are going to change in your college life. You will realize you now have a different taste in things than when you were in high school. This is totally fine; it means that you are maturing and figuring yourself out. This will lead to some uncomfortable dilemmas, however. You will realize some of those old high school friends are not as cool as you thought. The person you are dating is not who you once thought they were. They have changed, and so have you. This is a time of heartbreak and loss. Loss is not always bad; it means you have the opportunity to change going forward. Sure, it is okay to feel sad about these lost relationships. You cannot look to the past and reminisce. If you keep looking back at the people who are no longer in your life, you will miss out on the new people who want to be in yours now. Some people are not meant to stay in your life forever. This change allows you to appreciate the people who are in your life and to look forward to new people you will meet.

July 21st

"It is not death that you should fear, you should fear never beginning to live."

- Marcus Aurelius: Roman Emperor & Stoic Philosopher

Sometimes, we forget that we are mortal beings. It seems weird to say that we will die one day, but it is the truth. It is a hard truth to grasp when you are in college because it is hopefully far away. When you finally accept this, you start to realize how much time you wasted away doing nothing. Unfortunately, most people realize this when they are much older. They reflect back on what they did not do. Do not do this; rather, understand that your time is finite. Do the things you enjoy. You do not want to look back on your college career and wish you had done everything differently. Go out and enjoy life when you do not have a big test coming up. Go socialize with people. Go join the clubs and do the activities you were on the fence about doing. When you look back and think about college, you want to tell yourself that you regret nothing you did, and you experienced everything to its fullest.

July 22nd

"Kindness in words creates confidence. Kindness in thinking creates profoundness. Kindness in giving creates love."

- Lao Tzu: Ancient Chinese Philosopher

If you have already started your college experience, you know of the stresses that college throws at you. If you have not started college yet, be prepared for some pretty hard days. Because there are some days when everything goes wrong, you never really have any idea what someone else is going through. This is why you need to treat everyone with kindness. Everyone is fighting their own battles at college; this is why you need to be nice to everyone that you meet. Hold the door for people. Ask people to join your discussion group in class. These little gestures of kindness are a breath of fresh air for someone who has had a pretty rough day. Whether in college or not, we have all witnessed or experienced what it is like to have a bad day, and the people around making it worse. Spread kindness to everyone. You never know what kind of day they have had.

July 23rd

"No great thing is created suddenly, any more than a bunch of grapes or a fig."

- Epictetus: Ancient Greek Philosopher

Have you ever watched a flower grow? You plant the seed, water it, and leave it in sunlight. You check on it the next day, and it looks like nothing happened. Then in a few days, a little sprout has reached the top. It continues to grow in a few more days until it becomes a fully blossomed flower. This flower did not just sprout fully bloomed hours after it was planted. It took time for it to fully form into what it is now. The same can be said for your goals and aspirations; those goals and aspirations will not be completed in a single day. They will require a bit of patience and perseverance. You are not going to get a college degree in a day. But if you work at it each day, in a few years, it is totally possible. Nothing worthwhile can be completed quickly. Whatever your goal is, do not be discouraged if you do not see immediate results from it. It takes time for good things to fully develop. Trust the process because it makes the results so much sweeter when they finally bloom.

July 24th

"Nothing great in the world was accomplished without passion."

- Georg Wilhelm Friedrich Hegel: 19th Century German Philosopher

◆

You know what it is like to attempt something without passion. Growing up in school, you were often forced to participate in activities you did not have a huge passion for. If you do not like art, your paintings probably are not incredibly done. If you do not have a passion for reading, your reading list is probably rather small. There is no issue with not having a passion for everything; this makes us unique. It is always so surprising that you will talk to other people and find they have no real passion for anything. They went to college and chose some subject to study, not because they had passion for it or the jobs that came with it, but because it was one of the first choices on a list. No good will come from doing something without some passion behind it. Think of all the great contributions that artists have left humanity—they had to have some passion for that. To build giant skyscrapers, each of those builders and architects had to have at least some passion for it. Find what you are passionate about and follow that passion; it will lead you to great accomplishments.

July 25th

"A king's lot: to do good and be damned."
- Marcus Aurelius: Roman Emperor & Stoic Philosopher

You are the king of your own life, a sort of ruler of your destiny. A good king does what is best for his kingdom. You must do what is best for you. There will be people who criticize your choices, but they are not the rulers of your life. You know what is best for you, and you see the road that you must travel, even if everyone else does not. You might change your major and hear disapproval from the people around you about your new career path. There will be no shortage of people to tell you that you are wrong, or that you should do something different. Do not let their words dictate your choices. You are the ruler of your choices, and what you decide is what you will do. It can feel isolating to be the only person who thinks what you are doing is right. However, think about all the great figures in history. They were often criticized for what they did at the time. Only you see the full picture of your life and what you want to do. People will sometimes criticize your choices, but do not let them deter you from your success.

July 26th

"I like the dreams of the future better than the history of the past."

- Thomas Jefferson: 3rd President of the United States

It is easy to look back and regret the things we did. Maybe we did not try hard enough on a test or told others stuff we wished we had not. Looking back at your mistakes is a great way to figure out what you did wrong and learn from it. However, you cannot live in the past. If you continue to live in the past, you will beat yourself up over something that is already over. You will never have a better future if you cannot let the past go. You are a human being; you are going to make mistakes. Those mistakes have consequences, and sure, they suck. You will get over them eventually and learn from them, and this is when you need to use what you learned to help you in the future. Next time, you will spend more time preparing for that test and think twice about what you say to others. You never really learn from your mistakes if you can never move on from them. So, go ahead and feel sad and reflect on your mistakes for a little bit. Just do not keep living in the past, or you will never have a better future.

July 27th

"Thousands of candles can be lit from a single candle, and the life of the candle will not be shortened. Happiness never decreases by being shared."

- Buddha: Ancient Indian Religious Leader

Sadly, you will never get back most of the things you share with people. When you give your roommate the last package of ramen noodles, you will not get that package back. Most of the gifts we provide to friends and loved ones are freely given without expectation of repayment. Happiness is different. You are never short any less than what you started with when you give some away. You can give joy to as many people as you want, and it will never be something that you lose. When someone is having a bad day, your happiness might be why they get out of that bad day. Your joy can help cheer others up. Why would you not try to help others who have a bad day? Hopefully, you are a pretty happy person in life, so use that to make others happy. There is no limit to the people you can help. You will have some bad days at some point; hopefully, someone comes along and spreads the light of happiness in your life. You should do the same for others.

July 28th

"Many of life's failures are people who did not realize how close they were to success when they gave up."
- *Thomas Edison 19th Century American Inventor*

Unfortunately, too many people give up on their dreams when they were so close to accomplishing them. These people were one semester away from graduating college or a few more meetings away from their new business taking off. Why did they give up, you may ask? Because they felt that their goals were not reachable. This is really disappointing because they were so close to accomplishing some big things in their lives, but gave up because they did not know if they could do it. There are times when you will be tired, and you will begin to question whether or not you made the right choice to chase your goals. These are moments of doubt, and you have to push through these feelings and keep moving toward your goals. Oftentimes, the more you feel like giving up, the closer you are to having success. The failure is not that you failed; rather, you gave up on your goals and yourself.

July 29th

"No matter how difficult a task may look... Persistence and steady action will get you through."

- Lucretius: Roman Poet & Philosopher

We will all be faced with big tasks in life. Right now, for many of you, your big task is this semester of college. Between the many assignments, quizzes, readings, and exams, it can feel like a lot is being asked of you. You can, however, make the plan of success for your semester pretty simple. You are going to have times when you are thrown off course. Whether it is a problem in the classroom or outside. If you can maintain the same direction in your life, regardless of what happens, you will have success. Do not let the little mishaps deter you from continuing; it is just part of the journey. If you make time to work on your education each day, then you will have success. That might mean doing a few assignments or reading a few pages every single day. It might not be the most fun thing in the world, but it will help you out in the long run. As long as you stay the course and contribute to your studies every day, that large task of making it through the semester becomes much easier.

July 30th

"True life is lived when tiny changes occur."
- Leo Tolstoy: 19th Century Russian Writer

You are constantly changing as a person, whether you know it or not. You might not think that you have changed much from high school to now, but if you look back, you realize that gradually you, in fact, have changed. You are never going to stop changing. This can be a sobering realization. As much as you may like where you are in life, it too will also change. You should not be upset about these new changes because it has been happening your whole life. In high school, the people you hung out with will be different from those you hang out with in college. Subjects that interest you will also change. Sometimes it feels like you are changing so much that you do not even know who you are anymore. You get to experience all of these new changes and figure yourself out. You can try to fight this change, but it will happen eventually; it is often best to just ride with it and see where it takes you. These changes will lead you to some of the most exciting moments and people of your life, so go with it.

July 31st

"Pride goes before destruction, a haughty spirit before a fall."

- Proverbs 16:18

It is important to have some self-confidence in yourself. You should be confident in the person you are and the person you are becoming. With that being said, it is also important to not think too much of yourself. It is a fine line between self-confidence and cockiness, and it is a line that you have to walk carefully. Often, when people believe they are better at something than everyone else, it is not too long before they are humbled. You will have classes where one student believes that the course is just too easy or that they are some genius. Because they felt like this, they did not think they needed to study before the test. They had an insane amount of self-confidence to pass the test with no studying whatsoever. You can probably imagine how that ended for them. That student gets humbled pretty quickly, and they never talk about the class being too easy again the rest of the semester. It is often better to stay on the humbler side of things because you do not have such a hard fall in good or bad situations.

August

August 1st

"Progress is not achieved by luck or accident, but by working on yourself daily."

- Epictetus: Ancient Greek Philosopher

When you first start college, it is likely you will think it would be roughly the same difficulty as high school. Our high school teachers did tell us they were trying to prepare us for college. You will see that these thoughts are very quickly disproven. In most reputed colleges, you cannot skip class, ignore assignments, or underestimate tests and walk away with a passing grade. You are not going to accidentally get a college degree. There is a certain amount of work you will have to put in to succeed. Suppose you have goals of making the university honor roll. In that case, you will have to work every day on your classes to keep your grades high enough to obtain that goal. You are not going to just skate by on luck or accidentally get on the honor roll. You would not be as happy with yourself if you accidentally succeed rather than working hard for it. With most big goals in life, you will have to do something every day to chase those goals. Work on those goals daily, and the progress will follow.

August 2nd

"We are each of us stronger than we think we are."
- Marcus Aurelius: Roman Emperor & Stoic Philosopher

Did your partner break up with you? Or did you just bomb your midterm? At this point, you probably think your life is coming to an end. How will I ever recover from this, you may think to yourself. Well, the answer is rather simple. You just keep moving on. The sun will come up tomorrow, and you will have the opportunity to become a better person. Your life will not end because of one girl or guy. It also will not end because of one bad test grade. These trials give rise to the opportunity to become a better person. As you mourn the breakup, you become a stronger person; as you study the material, you become a stronger student. And in the end, when you look back on it, you realize that you managed to come through the situation all right. At this point, you really begin to see the strength that you developed to pull through in these situations. We are all bound to go through tough spells in life; they help us grow stronger and allow us to see the true strength we actually have within.

August 3rd

"The greatest glorious masterpiece of man is to know how to live with purpose."

- *Michel De Montaigne: 16th Century French Philosopher*

We all want to achieve something in our lives. When you enrolled, you had the goal of achieving success at college, hopefully in the form of graduating with a diploma in hand. It is easy to think about all the different things you will achieve someday. However, it is hard to think about those first steps you have to take to get on the right path to those things. Knowing your purpose will be the starting line of your quest for achievement. Having a feeling of purpose toward a goal drives someone to that goal. Not only does it drive them to that goal, but it also helps them to not get discouraged when failures and setbacks start to pop up. The purpose is almost like a shield that helps protect you from the bad and leads you toward your goals. Sit down and think about the driving purpose behind your goals. If your goal is to graduate college, your drive has to be to get good grades and finish school with enough credits to get that piece of paper. So go with purpose toward your goals.

August 4th

"In the middle of the journey of life I found myself within a dark woods where the straight way was lost."

- Dante Alighieri, 13th Century Italian Poet & Writer

Coming to a metaphorical fork in the road is something everyone has experienced in life. When you decide which way to go, you have to venture down that path and accept the consequences of that choice. Sometimes the effects are pretty good. Other times not so much. With many choices, you will have easy and hard options. You can take the easy path and have a better time, but the consequences usually suck. Or you can take the hard course, fight through the hardships you will encounter, and accept the much better results. Many people often take the easy path because it is easy. It requires very little work, and they do not have to worry about many hardships. They get to the end of their path and are usually disappointed with the results of their choice. Yes, it will be more difficult to go through the tough path, and there will be times when you will question why you went down this path. It will be so much more rewarding when you finish it, and you will be glad that you took that road.

August 5th

"Keep your attention focuses entirely on what is your own concern, and be clear that what belongs to others is their business and none of yours."

- Epictetus: Ancient Greek Philosopher

College is stressful, as you have already figured out. If you start worrying about other people's problems, you will just continue to stress yourself out. You already have enough to stress about between academics, friends, romantic relationships, internships, and everything else. It is hard enough not to get overwhelmed with everything you have going on in life. Focus on you and your problems. Only you can help yourself get through whatever you are going through. Sure, you can always lend a hand to help others, and they should do the same for you. That is just a helping hand; do not get involved in their business because it will start becoming your business. Minding your business will help ease the stress in your life because now all you have to worry about is you. We can all agree that it is easier to take care of one person rather than two. Getting involved in the drama of others often rarely ends well. It is never wrong to tell people that you just have too much on your own plate to get involved with their issues.

August 6th

"Is it so bad, then, to be misunderstood? Pythagoras was misunderstood, and Socrates, and Jesus, and Luther, and Copernicus, and Galileo, and Newton, and every pure and wise spirit that ever took flesh. To be great is to be misunderstood."

- Ralph Waldo Emerson: 19th Century American Philosopher

If you want to be great, you will notice how many people around you either settle for mediocrity or give up on their greatness. If you continue down your path of success, people will question why you are doing what you do. This is probably because they either quit or they settle and could not fathom why you would continue down such a difficult path. People are not going to always understand why you do what you do. When you stay in instead of party or read instead of play video games, you will get needled for it, but just think of the people who also felt this same pain. Some of the greatest minds in existence were not understood. If these greats can be misunderstood, then it is no surprise that you are too. Some people will not understand your reasoning to keep going, but the only person who needs to understand is you.

August 7th

"Be still like a mountain and flow like a great river."
- Lao Tzu: Ancient Chinese Philosopher

Life happens, and things will pop up that you were not expecting. These things that pop up are only a small portion of what you are actually experiencing. The majority of what will happen is how you will react to these events. A pretty good example of this is when class gets cancelled. This does not throw a huge wrench in your day when a class gets canceled. You are pretty happy about more free time, and you do not have to be in class. It happened out of the usual. It ended up not being too big of a deal because you had a positive attitude about it. When bad things happen, we tend to get more flustered about them, which causes them to become a bigger deal. Instead of becoming upset that something bad has come up in your day, it is often better to just go with the flow. Arguably, how we react to these events is the most significant part of the issue. Suppose you can respond positively and spin an unfavorable situation into something neutral or good. In that case, it makes your day even easier.

August 8th

"The will to win, the desire to succeed, the urge to reach your full potential... these are the keys that will unlock the door to personal excellence."

- Confucius: Ancient Chinese Philosopher

Good things come to those who wait. While this saying has some truth to it, there are times when you cannot sit around and wait. You need to go out and do. Being patient for success when you are working for it is good, but waiting around when you have not done anything will not lead to any results. You cannot sit around and wait for a college degree to come to you; you have to go out and work for it. If you want to start your own business, you cannot just wait for it to start; you have to go out and build at it. Sure, sometimes the good things take a while to come to light, but if you never start looking for them, then they will never show up. Go out today and start working for that college degree or start working to open your own business. You do not always need to be patient with what you want. There is no magic age for when it is best to start working toward your dreams. Start now. Be impatient to accomplish your goals because starting today gets you one step closer to completing them.

August 9th

"Acting on your anger makes everything worse than just feeling your anger."

- Marcus Aurelius: Roman Emperor & Stoic Philosopher

Nothing good has ever come from acting on something when you are angry. Your mind is too clouded with rage to act rationally. We have all been there before. You visit home and feel completely overwhelmed with school. You feel anxious, your head is spinning, and one of your family members is doing something that has pushed you past your limit. That feeling of anger is building up inside. Lashing out and causing a scene will only make you look bad and lead to hurt feelings. Rather, what should be done in this situation is when you feel the anger inside of you, you should think about the outcome of lashing out. Will you look like a fool? Will you offend everyone and hurt feelings? By thinking through these outcomes, you can now see that it might just be best to go outside and take some time to decompress. You can then go reevaluate the situation with a clear head. This will lead to better decisions and a lot less stress for yourself.

August 10th

"Life is very short and anxious for those who forget the past, neglect the present, and fear the future."

- Lucius Annaeus Seneca: Roman Stoic Philosopher

The consequences of mistakes are why we do not make those mistakes again. Putting your hand on a hot stove is why you do not ever put it back there again. Do not dwell on past mistakes, but rather use them as an opportunity to learn. Understand what you did wrong, and use it in the future. If you cannot do the things that need to be done today, you will always live with the anxiety of tomorrow. Some of the reasons people fear the future is because they have neglected the present. Suppose you do not pay any attention to the tasks you have at hand today. In that case, you will always be behind and anxious about tomorrow. If you can learn from past mistakes and give your attention to everything that must be taken care of today, then you should have no reason to fear the future. Everything will sort itself out if you stop making mistakes over and over and get your stuff done today.

August 11th

"If you want to be happy, be."
- Leo Tolstoy: 19th Century Russian Writer

It can be pretty easy to pin your happiness on outside events. Maybe you are only happy when your friend is happy or when your favorite sports team wins. Placing happiness on external events and things will usually lead to unhappiness. People and things are fallible, which means they will mess up or not do well. If you place your happiness on that, you are bound to be unhappy a lot. The only reliable person you can put your satisfaction on is you. You can make any situation better by being in a good mood. The external event is not necessarily good or bad; it is just how you perceive it to be. You might sense your favorite team losing as a bad thing, but that does not mean that it has to get your mood down. Is it disappointing that they lost? Of course it is. Do you have the ability to shake it off and not let that one thing ruin your whole day? Also, yes. No situation is as bad as what you think it is. You can change the way you look at life. You can look at it negatively and always be a negative person. You also could look at it more positively and be a happier person. Happiness is always better, just FYI.

August 12th

"A person's fears are lighter when the danger is at hand."

- Lucius Annaeus Seneca: Roman Stoic Philosopher

The summer before you go off to college, you might start to feel pretty anxious about all the new changes that are about to happen. You are going to be away from your family and friends for the first time. You may be balancing college courses with a job. Financial responsibilities are daunting enough, let alone mixing in a full semester of classes. You might feel some pressure to find new friends. There are plenty of reasons to feel anxious about your upcoming semester at college. The reason you feel anxious about these changes is because of the unknown aspect of it. You have probably never been on your own to know what you have to do. Nor have you ever been to a college class to know what to expect. You are going to go to college, and you will face all the situations you feel anxious about now. Most of the time, we exaggerate the things we feel anxious about. You will manage to balance your courses with your job and social life. The good news is that while you are anxious about everything now, when you get going in college, that anxiety will diminish.

August 13th

"Three things in the world worth having: courage, good sense, caution."

- *Hausa Proverb*

It is great to have many skills and values, but what would your top three be? Courage, good sense, and caution should be at the top. If you have these three virtues, you will be able to go through life with more ease than others. Having courage is something that will greatly benefit you in life. When you are trying to do something out of your skillset, having the courage to do it will make the difference. Being courageous will help you do better at bigger things, even if you are not ready. Having good sense is important because nothing can get you distracted if you have good, practical judgment. If something does not seem like a good idea, then do not do it. This brings us to caution. If you go through life throwing caution to the wind, you will end up crashing and burning, and it will not be fun. You do not need to be the most cautious person in the world, but if something does not feel right in your gut, it probably means it is not right. These three virtues are some that will help you through any situation that you encounter.

August 14th

"There is no illusion greater than fear."
- Lao Tzu: Ancient Chinese Philosopher

Have you ever thought about what it would be like to try something new, such as cooking, painting, or running? You have no idea if you would like it or not if you have never tried it. What is stopping you from trying it out - making a mistake? It does not matter if you make a mistake; you will not try painting for the first time and create an absolute masterpiece. You are probably going to fail the first time miserably. If you keep working on your painting skills every day, you will suck at it less and less. Would you rather go through life with a bunch of exciting new experiences with a few mistakes or a life with no experiences but no mistakes? Exactly, so do not give up on that recent activity you are thinking about trying. Go out and try it. You will make some mistakes, but eventually, you will improve and make fewer mistakes. Part of the learning curve of most things requires making mistakes and learning from them. Try out something new, and do not let the fear of making a mistake hold you back.

August 15th

"Putting things off is the biggest waste of life. It snatches away each day as it comes, and denies us the present by promising the future."

- *Lucius Annaeus Seneca: Roman Stoic Philosopher*

It would probably be a lie if we all said we have not procrastinated at one point or another in our lives. As some of us do under the pressure of quickly approaching due dates, this is not the best way to live. When you put off work until later, all you have done is put a cloud of anxiety over your head. This cloud will only follow you around and prevent you from enjoying yourself now. You know that you are going to have to get that project done or that paper written at some point or another. As each day passes and that due date gets closer, that cloud of anxiety gets darker. Why not just knock that paper or project out now? This would allow you to not void the present and allow you peace in the future. Plus, future anxiety will follow you if you put something off and try to go out and enjoy yourself. If you bite the bullet and get it done now, think of all the time you will have in the future to go enjoy yourself.

August 16th

"Do not go where the path may lead; go instead where there is no path and leave a trail."
- *Ralph Waldo Emerson: 19th Century American Philosopher*

Sometimes you should not follow everyone else and instead go your own way. A great example of this is when your high school friends decide to go to the same university, but you do not go there. Maybe the school you are going to only offers the major you want, or perhaps you are going on an athletic scholarship. Whatever the reason, you should not start to question whether to join the path of the many; instead, this is your chance to create your own way. Even in college, you will come across this dilemma. Whenever you feel that going with the majority is not the best option for you, start your own path. Life is too short to do what everyone else is doing. Once you create this path, it allows others to use you as a role model. This is usually the more fulfilling path that will lead to the highest happiness for you. When there is no best path for you to take, make one you feel confident about.

August 17th

"From good people you'll learn good, but if you mingle with the bad you'll destroy such soul as you had."

- Musonius Rufus: Roman Stoic Philosopher

Who are the people you are allowing into your life? Are these people inspiring you to do your best, or holding you back? If you surround yourself with good people, you will receive good from them. One of the best people you can surround yourself with are positive people. People who continuously inspire you and are in a good mood will affect you in these ways as well. People with good habits are the types of people to surround yourself with. Surrounding yourself with good habits will motivate you to pick up these good habits. You are going to lose the friends who do not want the best for you. You have to think about whether you want to surround yourself with people who do not want the best for you. Eliminating negative relationships and people from your life is another great way to surround yourself with more positive people. Be cognizant of the type of people you surround yourself with.

August 18th

"Discipline is the soul of an army. It makes small numbers formidable; procures success to the weak, and esteem to all."

- George Washington: 1st President of the United States

It is easy to choose what you can have now over what you want in the future. Going out to party now is easier than staying in to study for your test. Yes, it is more fun now to go to a party with your friends, but in the future, you will wish you would have studied for that test. It takes some discipline to put off the pleasures of now and hold out for what you really want in the future. If you really want to do well in school, you will need the self-discipline to make yourself study. Discipline is something you will have to work at. It does not come naturally to everyone. You are going to be given plenty of opportunities to work at it. You have to make a choice about what matters more to you, the now or the future. If you think the future goal is more important, then you will be willing to give up the pleasures of now for it. If you really want to obtain the joys of your future goals, you will need the discipline to stick to the future plans and not worry about the pleasures of now.

August 19th

"Live as if you were to die tomorrow. Learn as if you were to live forever."

- Mahatma Gandhi: 20th Century Indian Lawyer & Political Ethicist

---

Most of you would prefer not to die tomorrow. You are young and have a lot of life yet to live. Just as a thought experiment, if you were to exist tomorrow no longer, would you be satisfied with everything you have done? The answer is probably no. This should make you think about what you want to do in life and start doing it now. There is no better time to start than today. You never know what tomorrow will bring, so it is best to do all you can today. Lying around doing nothing will not make you feel like you are living life to your fullest. Go out and experience the world and meet different people. The other thing you cannot forget is to always learn something. You should try to learn one new thing every day. This should not be too hard of a challenge if you are in college. If you had eternity to live, you would try to take in as much information as possible. You would learn about the world and everything it has to offer. Unfortunately, you have a shorter time frame to learn everything in, so get busy living and learning.

August 20th

"To pursue the impossible is madness, and it is impossible for bad men to act in character."

- Marcus Aurelius: Roman Emperor & Stoic Philosopher

People change; we all know that. What you may never fully comprehended is how much some people can change and how quickly they can change. You will have people who are incredibly close to you and then become strangers the next day. Some people change for good, to better improve their lives and the ones around them. Others do not follow this path. Some people will change for the worse. This might be for several reasons, peer conformity being a big reason. Usually, some sort of intervention puts that person back on the right track. Others are just generally not good people. They do bad things just because they can. There are people for which you can be the hero and save them from going off the deep end. There are others who, by nature, you cannot save. Do not waste your time and effort on these people. Help the people who want to be helped; they are worth helping.

August 21st

"While we may not be able to control all that happens to us, we can control what happens inside us."

- Benjamin Franklin: 18th Century Writer & Inventor

Most of life is how you perceive it. You can have an optimistic or pessimistic view of everything. Most things in life are not that fun unless you look at them with an optimistic outlook. Waking up and going to class and studying all day does not sound like the most fun thing to do in the world. You can make it better if you look at it with some optimism. Think of how much better a person and student you become each day you go to class. The same thing can be said about your life in general. If you look at it pessimistically, it sounds pretty bad. You are born, go to school, work, and then you die. Yikes! You can look at it with an optimistic view and make the most of each day. You have to make each day worth it. It does not really matter what you do, as long as at the end of the day you can look back and be glad that you did it. It can be hard sometimes to make the best of a situation. Still, you will live a pretty miserable life if you cannot find good in anything. Make life worth living by finding the best of each day.

August 22nd

"God himself favors the brave."
- Ovid: Ancient Roman Poet

You are about to go through a period where you will probably experience low confidence. You are going to a brand-new school with all the new people around you. You are on your own. All of this can lead you to not have a lot of confidence in yourself. Times of low confidence call for a high amount of courage. Sure, you might not have a lot of experience doing these new things, but as long as you can attempt them courageously, you will have better success. You might not perfect these activities on the first attempt, but if you look at how you do them both courageously and not so much, you can guess which one will end up better for you. Once you have mastered these activities, you will be presented with different challenges as a new college student. These new challenges will be in things you have low confidence in because you have never done them before. You will never be short of times when you might not be very confident. You can make up for this with high confidence. If you are couragous, then you can do anything.

August 23rd

"It is not enough to be busy...The question is: what are we busy about?"

- Henry David Thoreau: 19th Century American Writer & Philosopher

---

Final projects in college are no joke. In high school, you might have had to make a small presentation, and you could probably finish the project in one night. College is a bit different because these projects are usually something you work on the entire semester; you just hand them in at the end. Not only are these projects long because they take an entire semester to complete, but they are usually pretty tedious as well. If you are looking at this project and have no idea where to start, the only recommendation for you is to find the smallest and easiest portion and start working on that first. If you can at least find something that you can complete, that at least gets the ball rolling. Once you succeed at that portion, you can move on to a bigger part of the project. You are breaking this big project down into smaller, more manageable pieces. Take a look at which small amount you can complete successfully and start there; everything else will begin to come together as you go along.

August 24th

"Fear is only as deep as the mind allows."
- Japanese Proverb

None of us want to live in fear; it takes a lot of energy and causes a lot of anxiety to live in this way. However, we make a lot of our decisions because we are fearful. When a close friend no longer goes out because they do not want to get heartbroken, this is an example of living in fear. You will find love at some point, but if you never go out and look for it, it can never find you. The same can be said for school. If your dream is to be a doctor, but you are too scared to take a really hard class in chemistry, then you will never have the opportunity to live out your dream. Your dreams should be something you follow, not something you hide away from. If you are passionate about your dreams, you will push fear aside and follow your calling. Living in fear will always inhibit you from your dreams. How are you going to accomplish anything if you are running away from your fears? Life is too short not to chase your dreams. Do not live in fear. It is time to go out and follow your dreams.

August 25th

"What does not benefit the hive does not benefit the bee either."

- Marcus Aurelius: Roman Emperor & Stoic Philosopher

Working with others is a situation you encounter many times in your life, whether it is in college, your job, or with your friends and family. You are going to have to learn how to work as a group. In college, this will most likely come in the form of a group project or presentation. These can be a real pain because you are relying on the work of others for your own grade. Probably the worst thing that you can do in a group project is not pull your own weight. No one likes the person who does not help, does not contribute anything to the project, and just hopes to coast off everyone else's work for a good grade. Your lack of work is only hurting the group as a whole. You have to be a good team player and understand that while your role may seem insignificant, it truly does play a part of a much larger project. Do not be the person who does not help the group out. Be the person who takes their share of the project and finishes it on time. Not only will your groupmates thank you, but your grade will too.

August 26th

"May you live all the days of your life."
- Jonathan Swift: 17th Century Irish Essayist & Poet

It can get pretty hard to make the most of each day when you are stuck in a rather boring schedule. If you wake up, go to class all day, eat dinner, and go to bed, it can be hard to find the good in mundane routines. You still need to look at the interests in your life and realize each day is special. If nothing else, just appreciate the fact that you are going to college. Sure, it feels like it is not good now, but take a step back and look at how few people go to college, all things considered. Appreciate the nice weather, the friends you made, and the attractive partner in your group project. Give each day a reason to be remembered. We do not live forever, so cherish your time where you are. A lot of people tell you to "enjoy your college years; you will never get them back." There is some truth to that, so make each day meaningful. Do whatever you can to fill your day with meaning. Plus, it is nice to look back and realize that you gave each day meaning.

August 27th

"The gem cannot be polished without friction, nor man perfected without trials."

- Chinese Proverb

It can often feel like the trials that we go through are unfair. These trials can feel like we are being punished or that nothing good could come from them. You need to realize that the trials and bad situations you go through can be very helpful. You must learn from these times to become stronger and smarter. You become stronger because these tough times make it so that there is no option for you other than to get stronger. If you can persevere through these moments, you will walk out a stronger person. It also can help you become smarter. Maybe you got yourself into these trialing times, or perhaps they just happened. Either way, there is something to be learned from it. If you did it yourself, then you could learn how to get out of this situation and how to never get back into a position like it. If it is just a bad situation that happened, it will teach you how to push past the bad and get to the good. These events will never go away; you must learn to go through them. These bad situations may seem bad, but they are just polishing you into a better person.

August 28th

"A man who does not plan long ahead will find trouble at his door."

- *Confucius: Ancient Chinese Philosopher*

When you are presented with a problem, how do you solve it? For most of us, the problems we encounter in college are pretty unique. They are more thought-provoking because they are problems that we have never had before, and we are old enough to fix them on our own. The best way to solve a problem is to think of what action you will take to correct the problem. It is almost impossible to fix a problem if you have no plan of attack. You cannot expect the pain of the problem to go away if you are doing nothing about it. You have to act on it. So, first, you must think about how you will fix this problem. The next thing you have to do is be constantly aware of your plan and change it accordingly. Are you looking for issues that come up or details that you missed from before? As you look at your problem, you must think about what you need to do next or how you can improve it. Do not act on a problem without thought, but also, think like a person who will work.

August 29th

"Not what we have but what we enjoy, constitutes our abundance."

- Epictetus: Ancient Greek Philosopher

Whether you go to a giant college with tens of thousands of students or a small college with only a few hundred, you are bound to find people who have stuff that you do not. Some might have nicer cars; others might have a designer wardrobe. The likelihood that you step foot on a college campus and have more than everyone else is staggeringly low. Do not let this get you down. It is not about what we do not have, rather what we do have. If you enjoy what you have, then you should feel contentment. It is normal for us to always want something. There will be plenty of times when you will see a cool car or cool pair of shoes and think, Man, I wish I had those. However, this is not a good way to live. If you always search for more than what you have, you will never be happy with what you have. It is an endless chase for more goods. Take a step back and look at how lucky you are to have all the stuff you already do. Enjoy the things you have, and be content with what you enjoy. Always chasing more will never lead to happiness, but enjoying what you already have will.

August 30th

"Believe you can and you're halfway there."
- Theodore Roosevelt: 26th President of the United States

Your track record with test taking is spotty at best. Hey, not everyone is a great test taker. The people who do poorly on tests do bad not only because they do not understand the material, but also because they do not believe they can take this test. If you do not believe in yourself, then who is supposed to? Whatever you are trying to accomplish, if you think that you can do it, more than likely, you actually can. You may not know if you will make good grades when you go to college. You might think that the classes are too big and would lead you to sink into mediocrity. It is good to realize before you started class that a negative way of thinking is the wrong way to go about your college career. If you begin to believe that you can do good in your classes, then you will rise above your expectations. You might just end your semester with the best grades of your life, which is no easy feat in college. You have to believe you are on your way to completing your new goals. Try really believing in yourself, and you will notice an improvement in all the things you do.

August 31st

"Crimes often return to their teacher."
- *Lucius Annaeus Seneca: Roman Stoic Philosopher*

We all know the saying: "What goes around comes around." Without us knowing, we often set the example to the people around us. Maybe you have younger siblings or friends who look up to you. When you lie, are dishonest and deceitful, that is the standard you have shown the people around you to be. Do not be surprised that when you are untrustworthy with a friend or sibling, they will be the same way back to you. You can change this by showing the opposite traits to the people around you. If you are honest and truehearted to the people around you, they will become the same way back. We all would rather have people be real with us instead of deceitful. Project onto others the type of treatment you would want to get back. Do not be surprised when you set a bad example for the people around you that it comes back to bite you. The same can be said with good examples, but what comes back to you will be more pleasant.

September

September 1st

"When you arise in the morning, think of what a precious privilege it is to be alive - to breathe, to think, to enjoy, to love."

- Marcus Aurelius: Roman Emperor & Stoic Philosopher

───────────────◆───────────────

We can all get caught up in the turmoil of our very busy lives. Once college classes start, you will quickly find out that you are in for some very busy weeks. It is no surprise that we take a lot for granted when we are this busy. However, you should take some time to acknowledge how amazing it is to be alive and to be you. There are so many things we do and see every day that we never stop to think about the pleasure it is to experience. You may even pass by things on a day-to-day basis that do not register as being a privilege to witness every day, whether it be seeing the sunrise or the majesty of an ivory-covered lecture hall. Enjoy every breath, thought, and emotion you experience because you may never get to again. Like the quote says: You get to breathe, think, enjoy, and love. These are some of the most amazing things you can do. And just think, you can do all of these things in one day in college. Never take for granted how awesome it is to be you and all you get to experience at college.

September 2nd

"Perfection is attained by slow degrees; it requires the hand of time."

- Voltaire: 18th Century French Writer & Philosopher

A seed does not grow into a plant without some work. It takes a lot of hard work to grow from a tiny shell into something much bigger and more beautiful. You can think of your path to success like that of a seed. If you plant it and give it water and sunlight, it will start to grow, but it will take some hard work from that seed to become the blossom. You will not have success if you do not work hard at it. That might mean having to do some things that are outside of your comfort zone. You will have to make some sacrifices if you are serious about accomplishing your dreams. None of those things are easy to do. That is why they are called hard work. Success will start to show when you start working hard. Just because you work hard for a little bit does not mean that you are going to see instant results. Good things take some time. If you can do the hard work and give yourself time, you will see the success.

September 3rd

"The roots of education are bitter, but the fruit is sweet."

- Aristotle: Ancient Greek Philosopher

Listen, school sucks sometimes. It is a lot of studying and reading and testing. Doing all of that day after day really starts to wear you out. These things especially suck when you know that your friends are having fun and you are stuck under a lamp reading a book. The good news is that the payoff for your hard work with your studies is great. The harder work you put into studying, the richer the fruits of your labor. Think about this in sports terms. If you never practice shooting or dribbling a basketball, how good will you do in a game? Not very good. Now imagine that you practice for several hours a day on shooting and ball-handling drills. You will do much better this way. Most college students replaced shooting and dribbling with note-taking and studying. The more work you put into the boring and not fun parts, the better the reward will be. So, while it sucks now, you will be glad that you put in all that hard work because the payoff will be well worth it.

September 4th

"If you are irritated by every rub, how will your mirror be polished?"

- Rumi: 13th Century Persian Poet

College is a process; it is not something that you can complete overnight. Just like with any procedure, there is a grind that you have to go through to be successful and make it. Nothing good ever comes easy, right? If you really want to graduate, then you will have to commit to the process. This is not a process where you get to pick and choose when you want in and out of it. You cannot go to college for the fun parties and not for the classes; how will you graduate if you do? If you cannot commit to the whole process, good and bad, you will never accomplish anything. The greatest things did not happen perfectly; there are going to be some bumps along the way. You just have to make sure you can persevere and get over them. You have to really want something to endure the bad and ride with the good. There will be some sacrifices made along the way. You have to decide if your goal is important enough to make those sacrifices worth it.

September 5th

"I failed my way to success."
- Thomas Edison 19th Century American Inventor

Very rarely will you ace every single assignment, quiz, test, or project that you get assigned. If you do, that is awesome, but that is a rarity. We all have different definitions of "failing" something in college. For some, failing an assignment actually means getting an F. For others, it might mean getting a B. No matter what your definition is, you are inevitably going to "fail" in one of your classes. That is totally fine because it allows you to learn. You will figure out what you need to do better next time to not fail. It might mean taking better notes or spending more time preparing. If you do this, then you will ultimately succeed in your class. Do not get so down on yourself for failing because we all do at one point or another. Feeling bad that you failed is normal, but do not constantly feel bad that you failed at something. Rather, use it as a platform to boost yourself up to the heights of success. If you fail enough times, then you will eventually find the way to have success.

September 6th

"To love oneself is the beginning of a lifelong romance."
- *Oscar Wilde: 19th Century Irish Poet*

College can be pretty stressful. There are times when it feels like all you do is study and sleep. If anyone does that for more than a week, they will be pretty dejected. You need to make sure that you take care of yourself as well. Take care of the big three pieces of you: physical, mental, and spiritual. Take good care of your body. It is the only one you have. Go for a walk and get out in the sunlight. Make sure to eat foods that are good for you. Help your body out, and it will help you back. Have some hobbies or activities that you can do to help relieve stress. Take some time to relax and do something you want to do. Watch a movie or hang out with friends. These small things can really make a difference in your life. Your spiritual health is one that many people forget. It is just as important as the other two. Pick up meditation or just sit in a quiet room for a few minutes. Connect with a community of faith, a place where you and others of a shared belief can get together. Take care of these three pieces, and your life will be better.

September 7th

"Dig inside yourself. Inside there is a spring of goodness ready to gush out at any moment, if you keep digging."

- *Marcus Aurelius: Roman Emperor & Stoic Philosopher*

There is good within each one of us. The world can be a pretty cruel place, which can make it hard to be inherently good to others. There will be times when you might be tempted to do something that is not good. When you feel tempted, you should evaluate why you feel like doing less than what is good. It is in this moment of reflection that you should look within yourself to find the good you are capable of showing. You have to be honest with yourself about what it will take to show goodness to the world. It might require getting rid of some toxic friends or breaking a bad habit. The world becomes better when everyone does good to one another. You can have trusting relationships and peace with those around you. There will be people who will try to take advantage of the goodness you show. There will always be some bad people, but you cannot let this halt your goodness to the world.

September 8th

"Who sees all beings in his own self, and his own self in all beings, loses all fear."

- Hindu Scripture

Fear is the roadblock of most things we want to do in life. If you are frightened by something, you most likely will not attempt doing it. While this might have worked well for our primitive ancestors, it does not work well today. If you are scared of talking to new people, you most likely are not going to put yourself in situations where you have to meet new people. However, this is exactly what you need to do. If you are scared of talking to new people, go to a place where you are forced to talk to new people. You will notice that you get less and less scared of it when you start doing it. What are some things you have always wanted to do that you are too frightened to try? You should go and try it because you will notice that when you make up your mind that you are going to try, the fear begins to disappear. Fear leaves when it is no longer a mystery what you are getting yourself into. Sure, it might seem pretty scary now, but when you start trying it, you will forget why you were even scared in the first place.

September 9th

"Do not be afraid; our fate cannot be taken from us; it is a gift."

- Dante Alighieri: 13th Century Italian Poet & Writer

The great thing about life is that you make your own fate. Your choices create consequences, which leads to the construction of your future. This is why fate is a gift. You are constantly building it, and working towards your future. The choices you make now are what create the road to everything you will do and will happen to you in the future. You may worry that you are not making the right choices, or that you feel you have to choose a certain path in life. Fate is what you are meant to do. This knowledge of fate should make you feel better about the choices you make because you are always going to choose the right option. No matter what set of options you choose, it will still lead you down a road you have created. Worry about what you can control, since this will lead your fate, and stop worrying about what you cannot control. These extraneous events will not be a major role in the fate you create. Extraneous events may seem like they will destroy the road you have created, but they are merely a road bump on your quest with fate.

September 10th

"The rich man is he who is content with what he has."

- Epictetus: Ancient Greek Philosopher

On campus you will immediately notice the difference in wealth among the students. Some will drive brand-new luxury vehicles; others will drive cars that barely have a functioning motor. Some will wear designer clothes; others will not. You cannot judge a person on their wealth based on their possessions. Some very rich people do not live in mansions or drive brand-new cars. The rich are those who are happy with what they have. If all you need to be satisfied is a small apartment, a couple friends, and an old but functional car, then, my friend, that is true wealth. The best kind of wealth is the wealth of life, not money. Find what you are content with and stick with that. You will realize that you will have true happiness when you can be happy with what you have, not the newest model of car or jacket. If you continue to chase the latest item, so you feel cool, you will never be happy. You are just chasing an unobtainable dream. True wealth is found in that which you feel most content with.

September 11th

"Time is the most valuable thing a man can spend."
- *Theophrastus: Ancient Greek Philosopher*

If you look at your friend in class who just aced their test, you might see someone who just is overly smart in that subject. You do not know what went on while you were not looking. Your friend was preparing for this test from the first day you went over the material. They did all the homework and even did some work on their own to get better at it. They went to the professor's office hours and asked questions to get a more personal understanding of the information. They quizzed themselves constantly, so it became almost second nature during test time. So, while you think they just got lucky, it was actually a countless number of hours spent perfecting their knowledge on this test. It is usually what we do not see that is the most important to success. While no one is looking, what you do will help prepare you for the big moment. This is true for sports, school, anything. Enjoy the work when no one is looking. This is when the most progress toward success is made.

September 12th

"It is time you realized that you have something in you more powerful and miraculous than the things that affect you and make you dance like a puppet."

- Marcus Aurelius: Roman Emperor & Stoic Philosopher

We have all been in situations where you feel like you are nothing but a face in a crowd. College can be especially challenging for this reason. Because if you were good at something in high school, the likelihood of someone being equal, if not better than you, in college is pretty high. If you were a good athlete in high school, chances are there is probably someone else who is even greater. If you were a valedictorian in high school, chances are high that someone else at your college was too, maybe on your dorm floor. Whatever it may be, it can feel like there is nothing special about you when you are surrounded by so many people. However, there is something special about you. This is one of the greatest times in your life to experiment and figure out what makes you special. Something is driving you inside. Take the time to listen to what it is moving you toward. You may be surprised at what your true calling in life is.

September 13th

"You may never know what results come of your action, but if you do nothing there will be no result."
- Mahatma Gandhi: 20th Century Indian Lawyer & Political Ethicist

---

A large part of college is learning. You know, that is what the whole point of college is. Part of learning is going out of your comfort zone and expanding your understanding of different subjects. Most people do not like to leave their comfort zones because it is new and uncomfortable. If to learn in one of your classes, you have to get up in front of everyone and work out a problem, will you do it? There are three options here. You can go up and do a problem for everyone and succeed at that problem, and you now know how to do that problem. Second option, you go up and fail the problem, and then you accept your failure and take it as an opportunity to succeed in the future. Or the third option, you do not go up in front of everyone and show that you can do the problem. In that last one, you have not shown anyone, including yourself, what you are capable of. Yes, you will fail sometimes, but you may also succeed. You will never know unless you go out and try.

September 14th

"I love those who can smile in trouble."
- Leonardo Da Vinci: 15th Century Italian Polymath

Looking at this giant project that you have to do, the last thing you will do is smile. Think how quickly you get a project done depends fully on your attitude to it. If you are nervous or do not want to do the project, it will take you a lot longer to finish it. If you are not excited to do something, chances are you will put off doing it. It helps to try looking at it in a positive light. Be happy that you get to do this project. Or just be satisfied that the sooner you do it, the sooner it is done. It might not be the most fun thing that you will do, but maybe smiling your way through will get you through it. So, smile at that giant project in front of you because you are happy that you are getting to do such a large project. You can use this with anything. Smile at your exams and quizzes. You will do better when you have those good hormones flowing through your brain. Smiling causes those good hormones, so help yourself, and you can do pretty well in college smiling your way through.

September 15th

"To love only what happens, what was destined. No greater harmony."

- Marcus Aurelius: Roman Emperor & Stoic Philosopher

Sure, we have all had times where we wished we had done something differently or had a different outcome. Maybe you wished you had tried harder on that test. Perhaps you wanted more people to like you at that party. We are never at a loss of "what could have been" thoughts. You need to start thinking that you have a unique road for your life. You do not need to do everything like everyone else does. If you did, then how would you be unique? Your path is like none other; this is the destiny you have created. Find the good in your situation. It might just be that this point in your journey is the tough stretch. You are bound to find some interest in your journey. Find it and appreciate it. This is your own special road that you get to climb. It can be hard not to look and see what others have and not feel some envy. If it is meant to be, it will also come to you. Every event and action have led you here, by your own doing. Love what you have done and what you are about to do.

September 16th

"Beware the barrenness of a busy life."
- Socrates: Ancient Greek Philosopher

We all want to have a successful college experience. This means doing as many things as you can. This can lead you to get spread pretty thin for your time. You have to plan your week of classes and when to study and spend time doing homework in advance. You plan when you can work and then figure out all the little jobs of being an adult like grocery shopping and doctors' appointments all before it happens. You feel like you have created such a busy schedule that you have no time to enjoy the moment you are in. There is nothing wrong with having a busy schedule. What you do not want to do is create such a busy schedule that you are unable to stop and live in the moment from time to time. The chase of future events leaves you unable to enjoy the present. While you work to prepare for future events, you miss the opportunity to live right now. What you do not want to do is become so focused on your busy life that you do not realize where the time went.

September 17th

"The more sand has escaped from the hourglass of our life, the clearer we should see through it."

- Niccolò Machiavelli: 16th Century Italian Diplomat & Philosopher

---

As you go through your college career, you will not only learn a lot in the classroom but equally as much outside. You will make mistakes your first year. You can look back later and laugh because you learned that lesson your first year, and when you are older you realize how stupid of a mistake it was. The older you get, the more sense these lessons make. It is because, with age, you just experience more. In your junior year, you will have had much more life experience than freshman you. When older, you will be able to think back on these lessons and apply them again, but as a freshman, you have not even encountered these lessons yet. It is okay to make mistakes as long as you learn from these mistakes. The lessons learned will help you in the future. We are all human and will make mistakes, so do not beat yourself up for making one. As long as you can take a lesson away from it, you will be able to apply it to similar future instances, and you will not slip up again.

September 18th

"We acquire the strength we have overcome."
- Ralph Waldo Emerson: 19th Century American Philosopher

It is easy to look around at some of your peers and wish for their lives. Maybe you are in a really intense course that requires a lot of time to prepare outside of class, while your friend has a pretty relaxing semester. This is not to say your friend will be unsuccessful, but instead of wishing your life was easier, you should rather want to be better. If you continue to push yourself and be better, you will eventually become better. Doing all your work, and then some, is a great way to become better at your intense class. Pretty soon, you might have mastered all the concepts, and your life becomes a lot less stressful. It did not get easier; you just got better. Pushing yourself allows you to find out how tough you really are. You become tougher in order to complete what you have to. If you wanted everything to get easier, you would just become softer. Instead of thinking about how easy some people have it, look at what you can do to become better, so maybe at some point, you make what you are doing look easy too.

September 19th

"In your life, don't be all about business."
- Marcus Aurelius: Roman Emperor & Stoic Philosopher

You have been told that the reason you are at college is to study and get a degree, not to party. While there is truth to this, if you spend all of your time in a library reading and studying, you will have a pretty miserable experience. Finding the medium between studying all day and partying all night is a fine but important line to walk. Enjoying yourself while maintaining high enough grades to not flunk out is important. College is stressful, and if you do nothing but feed the madness of academics, you will go crazy. Find hobbies and activities that you like doing to relieve some stress from your day. Even little things, like moving to another room to get a different view could be enough to help you. There is no end to the possibilities of fun activities that you can do during college. College is not all about working on your studies. It is about having some fun too. Make sure you give yourself the opportunities to enjoy life while at college. You will look back and be glad that you worked some fun activities into your life while you did.

September 20th

"If they spit at you behind your back it means you're ahead of them."

- Confucius: Ancient Chinese Philosopher

People are always going to talk behind your back and do things you will not like. It can become pretty distracting, always worrying about what other people are saying and doing behind your back. It can also be pretty hurtful to think about. When someone does something behind your back, you have to realize the direction they are going compared to where you are going. If they are behind you, then that means that you have surpassed them in life; that is why you have to look back to see what they are doing and saying. This should make you feel at least a bit better about this if it is happening to you, knowing that you are ahead of these people who are spreading rumors and gossiping about you. You have higher goals and aspirations in life than settling for that. Stop being concerned with what these people say and do because they are obviously not doing that much to better themselves or the world around them. You can take pride in knowing that you will not have to worry about these people soon because you will be so far ahead of them in life that you cannot see them when you look back.

September 21st

"Friendship is the source of the greatest pleasures, and without friends even the most agreeable pursuits become tedious."

- St. Thomas Aquinas: 13th Century Italian Philosopher & Catholic Priest

---

College is a great time for branching out in all aspects. Not only are you branching out your education, but you are also branching out socially. College can be a tough transition if you do not have many friends coming with you from high school. This can lead you to feeling pretty lonely. You should not feel upset about this, because this is a great opportunity. This new opportunity is making new friends. It can be hard to make new friends in college because you feel like you will forget your old ones. You might not be as close with your old friends as you once were, but you will always have that bond with those friends. They would not want you to feel lonely at school and would probably encourage you to meet some new people. Making friends in college is awesome; you get to meet different people from different backgrounds and interests. They understand the hardships of college because they are right there. If you are in the same boat as someone, you might as well fish together.

September 22nd

"Begin to weave and God will give the thread."
- German Proverb

There is no better time to start what you want to do than now. You are relatively young and free and feel like you can do anything. So, use that to your advantage and go out and start doing all the things you want to accomplish. Maybe it is a large accomplishment like earning a college diploma or starting a business. It could also be relatively small, like working out more or making new friends. Whatever it is, you might be wondering when the best time to start is, how you should start, and many other questions. The best way to find out is to just start. You will figure it out as you go. There is a higher power watching over you, and it will see when you need help. If you start working toward getting a college degree, you will see some divine help to complete your goals. If you think that you are alone in this journey of yours, then you would be wrong. As long as you start putting in the effort, there will be someone watching you to make sure that you stay afloat.

September 23rd

"One word frees us of all the weight and pain in life. That word is Love."

- Sophocles: Ancient Greek Tragedian

What do you love? You might think of a person that you love, or you may think of something you like doing. Both of these are necessary to have in order to help soothe the pains that we will encounter over our lives. When you love something, it helps ease the pain of life. There are multiple kinds of love. You do not love a family member the way you love a book or song. The love of a family member allows you to lift the pain of being alone. A friend's love can grant us momentary peace from the world's issues. Your love of a particular music or book genre helps you drown out the issues of the world with lyrics and pages. You may love watching a sport on television or a certain type of movie. All of these different variations of love allow us to bear the problems of the world. Finding things and people that you love makes life much more bearable. Bad things are going to happen to you, and you have to find the things and people you can surround yourself with that makes the bad things in life better. What will make the bad things in life better is your commitment to love.

September 24th

"First have a definite, clear practical ideal; a goal, an objective. Second, have the necessary means to achieve your ends, wisdom, money, materials, and methods. Third, adjust all your means to that end."

- Aristotle: Ancient Greek Philosopher

So, you just met with your advisor about enrolling in next semester's classes. You are no longer sure if this major is what you want to persue so you change to another major. Before doing this, you need to plan. You need to lay out a clear goal of what you want to major in, why this major will benefit you, and how long you are giving yourself to complete it. After you create your plan, you need to acquire everything you are going to need to achieve your new goal. This means notifying your advisor of the change in majors and getting a new degree schedule. You need to make sure you are financially prepared in case you need to take an extra semester or two of classes. It would not hurt to meet with some students who are currently in your new major to discuss the best way to start your new major. Once you have everything planned and figured out, it is time to begin your adventure in this new major.

September 25th

"Waste no more time arguing what a good man should be. Be one."

- Marcus Aurelius: Roman Emperor & Stoic Philosopher

Probably more than ever, we humans seem to not get along. Too many people are arguing over what should be done and what should not be done. From friends arguing about plans all the way up to government officials, it is noticeable that people tell each other what they think they should do but will not embody that idea themselves. Rather than telling one another what it means to be a good person, we should try to represent it by acting that way. Too many people are becoming hypocritical of what they want from others but will not first do it themselves. It is ignorant to tell people how they should act without first taking a look at themselves. Look at what you want out of others and think about how you can start doing it yourself. You may not be able to make other people good, but you can make yourself a good person. The world's problems will not fix themselves by pointing fingers at one another. Rather, we should all start representing what we think is an ideal way to act.

September 26th

"If you hate a person, then you're defeated by them."
- Confucius: Ancient Chinese Philosopher

As you know, bad things are bound to happen. Sometimes those bad things are caused by other people. If someone does you painfully wrong, it is normal to hate that person. Hate is a pretty powerful feeling to have for someone. If you hate someone, you probably have a very good reason to feel that way. Sometimes this feeling can cloud what we actually dislike. Do you hate the person, or do you just hate the thing that they did? Sometimes it can be pretty hard to distinguish which one you actually dislike. It is good to have some introspection into what you truly hate. No one is in a position to tell you that you should not hate anyone, because we have absolutely no idea what they did to you. What you should try is taking a step back and taking a good look at the person and the problem. Suppose you can separate person and situation and determine which one you hate. In that case, you will better understand what the actual issue is. You may realize that you do not hate the person; you just hate the problem they produced. This can help to rebuild bonds with these people.

September 27th

"Knowing is not enough; we must apply. Wishing is not enough; we must do."

- Johann Wolfgang Von Goethe: 18th Century German Poet & Playwright

---

If you want something in life, you will have to go after it. You cannot bet that what you want will just be gifted to you because the odds are stacked against you on that one. If you're going to get a good grade on this upcoming test, you will have to study and take notes and work at getting this good grade. How are you going to know if that guy or girl across the room is into you unless you go ask? If you never ask them, then that is always a rejection. The worst thing that can happen is that they say no, so go over and talk to them. There is a road to success in everything that you do. We all start somewhere, and we just have to keep moving to get to the finish line. How will you get to your goals if you never take that first step forward? Sure, it is a scary journey because you do not know what to expect. That is part of the fun that you have no idea what to expect with this. You have to have faith in yourself to keep walking forward and face whatever hardships are thrown your way.

September 28th

"Be not afraid of going slowly; be afraid only of standing still."

- Chinese Proverb

There is never any problem with taking your time as long as you continue to move forward. Not everyone will graduate college in four years. If it takes you an extra semester or two to graduate, it takes you an additional semester or two. There is no issue with that as long as you eventually get that degree. If it takes you a little longer to pick up on a concept in class, as long as you do not quit, then it will end well. Sometimes slow is the way to go. Rather than rushing through things, it is good to take your time and do a thorough job. When you take your time, you do not make as many mistakes because you are going slow enough to recognize them. You will have friends and peers who will graduate before you and get jobs before you. You cannot compare yourself to them. The only person you need to worry about is yourself. As long as you never stop, then you will be fine. Stopping is the worst thing you can do because it means you are closer to quitting than moving forward. Keep chugging along, even if it takes you longer, and you will eventually accomplish what you want.

September 29th

"It never ceases to amaze me: we all love ourselves more than other people, but care more about their opinion than our own."

- *Marcus Aurelius: Roman Emperor & Stoic Philosopher*

Each of us will do different activities to make us happy throughout the day. Sometimes it is watching some TV after studying for a bit. Other times it is going out to eat somewhere you really like. We treat ourselves better than we treat other people because we love ourselves. It is human nature to be more selfish toward yourself than others because others are not you. We will do stuff to make us happy, but will we care more about what others think? We care more about what others think of us than we do of ourselves. If you love yourself so much, why do you constantly fill your mind with worry and anxiety over what others are thinking about you? This seems a little backward to me. At the end of the day, your own happiness matters more than what others think about you. Enjoy the things that make you happy; do the activities that bring you joy. Do not care what others think or say about you, because why do their opinions really matter?

September 30th

"Always bear in mind that your own resolution to success is more important than any other one thing."

- Abraham Lincoln: 16th President of the United States

What does success mean to you? For some it is getting a college degree and then off to a big job with a huge paycheck. For others it might mean being the first in their family to attend college and to make enough to keep their family out of bankruptcy. No one person's definition of success is the right one. Some people are going to tell you what you have to do in order to reach their idea of success. It is not your job to live by other people's advice on success. You get to determine what success is. If success is being the first person in your family to complete college, then you have to do whatever it takes to become successful. You have come up with the idea of what having success looks like; you have made success a goal. Now you have to go and do whatever it is that you must in order to obtain this goal. People will try to change your mind to their own ideas of what success is for you. Ignore them and focus on what success means for you, and do what you must.

October

October 1st

"The noblest question in the world is: What good may I do in it?"

- Benjamin Franklin: 18th Century Writer & Inventor

We all have our reasons for choosing to do the things we do. You are choosing to major in something in the hopes of making a good living and having a good life. Here is a bit of advice for you: go and do some good in the world as you are concurring your dreams and goals. Your dreams and goals might be only about yourself, which most of them should be. Along the way, if you come across the opportunity to do good, then take it. It might not be the most glamourous gesture of your goodwill, but every little bit makes life better. When someone does some good to you, you feel pretty good the rest of the day. The person who did good also felt pretty pleased about themselves too. So, it is a win-win situation for everyone involved. Can you imagine how much better it would be if everyone tried to do good in the world? You always have the option of doing good. Go out and start working toward your goals. Just stop once in a while, look around, and see if you have the opportunity to do good for someone. You will make their day as well as your own.

October 2nd

"Life is ours to be spent, not to be saved."
- D.H. Lawrence: 20th Century English Writer & Poet

Life is not like money. You cannot save it and come back to it later. Once this day is over, it is over forever. That is kind of scary and sad to think about. That is why you need to make sure you never waste a day in your life. You have a finite number of days to live, especially days in college, so make the most of them. Go party with your friends, spend a day watching movies all day, and whatever else your mind can think of. Looking back, you do not want to regret wasting all those days in college. This also does not mean partying every day in college, because that wastes time getting your degree. And wasting time is just wasted days. Find the happy medium to have great memories and a college diploma. Just because you have to go to class on some days does not mean you cannot make memories; you can still meet your friends and study together or even just get some food. You will be glad that you started spending those days making memories rather than wasting them away.

October 3rd

"The individual has always had to struggle to keep from being overwhelmed by the tribe. If you try it, you will be lonely often, and sometimes frightened. But no price is too high to pay for the privilege of owning yourself."

- Friedrich Nietzsche: 19th Century German Philosopher

If you grew up in a small town, you probably have a reputation based on your last name, for better or for worse. You might feel like you have no way of being your own individual person because of the legacy your family holds in your town. Now, you are no longer in your parents' house and no longer in your hometown. You are no longer seen as only the offspring of your family; you are a unique individual. You are now free to choose and do whatever it is that you want to become. You do not have to follow in the family footsteps of life if you do not want to. Go find what interests you, and study what you have a passion for. You can be proud of your family name and legacy, but do not be afraid to blaze your own path in your life.

October 4th

"An investment in knowledge pays the best interest."
- Benjamin Franklin: 18th Century Writer & Inventor

You are going to get more knowledge. More specifically, you are going to college to understand specific subjects. It is easy to think that college will be the smartest you will ever get. You might have the belief that "Once I graduate, this will be the smartest I ever am. Everything from here is just using what I know." You can argue that this is not a good way to continue with your life. This is a pretty selfish belief to think that you are smart enough for the rest of your life. While it feels like a chore in college to learn, do not let it stop you from continuing to learn throughout life. Whether you are just starting college or have been out for decades, you can continue to improve your knowledge. When you get a job, you can keep learning and perfecting how you do your job. You can pick up new hobbies that interest you and learn about them. You will end up living a pretty boring life if you stop wanting to learn new things. Continue to seek out knowledge because it always beats out ignorance.

October 5th

"In a little while you will have forgotten everything; in a little while everything will have forgotten you."

- Marcus Aurelius: Roman Emperor & Stoic Philosopher

It is sometimes a relief to realize we do not remember everything that has ever happened to us in life. This allows us to let go and forgive ourselves of some of the guilt or shame from past mistakes. Whatever you did in the past that you regret or wish you did better, it will soon be forgotten. This lets you not hold on to the past and live clearly in the present. Do not let the fact you made mistakes in the past hold you back from trying something now. The same can be said about the future. We should not live in fear of what others will think or say and mistakes that can be made in the future. Because soon, this will become the past, and all will be forgotten. This really puts life into perspective. Do not overthink the past or future because it will soon not matter. Let this be a relief that you do not have to live in anxiety about every single thing in your life. Forgive what has happened, accept what will be, and live your life in the present.

October 6th

"Rejoice while you are alive; enjoy the day; live life to the fullest; make the most of what you have. It is later than you think."

- Horace: Ancient Roman Lyric Poet

This book talks a lot about planning your future. While this is good to do, you cannot just live in the future; you need to be here in the present. You will never get another today; once it is done, it is gone in the past. You do not want to be so focused on the future that you forget to enjoy what you have now. Some people are so obsessed over getting married in the future that they do not enjoy the person they are with right now. It is okay to just enjoy where you are right now. You will not stay in this one spot forever; life will keep moving forward. Before you start your march ahead, take a second to look around and enjoy all those people you have by your side, and enjoy the day for what it gives you. It is okay to not always have your future planned out and live one day at a time. There are going to be times when that is all you can do. So, enjoy life one day at a time, and enjoy what each of those days gives you. Every day has something special, so appreciate and enjoy it.

October 7th

"No human thing is of serious importance."
- Plato: Ancient Greek Philosopher

Of course, everything you are doing or going to do has some level of importance. What TV show you are going to watch tonight or what you will eat for dinner are pretty low importance. What career you will do for the rest of your life is a pretty high priority. However, do not worry too much about these decisions. Sure, they will have to be made at some point, but do not spend time torturing yourself thinking about every important decision you will ever have to make. Everything that you do is temporary. Some things you do will last longer than others. This should make you feel better, knowing that mostly everything bad you have done will disappear. It also means that those important decisions you have to make will disappear, too, one day. It is sad to think about, but you are not a permanent figure on this planet. This should bring some comfort, knowing that all those high-importance decisions and responsibilities will one day be gone. Take your choices seriously, but do not worry too much because they will not last forever.

October 8th

"The best way to predict your future is to create it."
- Abraham Lincoln: 16th President of the United States

Let us say, for example, you are a college freshman, and your goal in life is to become a doctor. You can see that you will be working in a hospital in your future and saving lives. College might be a lot tougher than what you had expected. Perhaps you are still hoping to be a doctor someday but are unsure what to do. Well, you need to start working on that now. You need to start enrolling in more science classes and making good grades. If you begin to create the goal of becoming a doctor now, it is more likely to turn out that way in the future. So, go out and keep working on your academics and meet people with the same goal as you. Maybe look into some clubs that relate to the healthcare field, or get a part time job in a clinic. If being a doctor is really what you want to do, you have to start preparing now. The only way to be something in the future is to start working at it now. Because the more prepared you are for it, the more likely it will become a reality.

October 9th

"Don't explain your philosophy. Embody it."
- Epictetus: Ancient Greek Philosopher

Are you going to change your major? Maybe you are going to start a new business? Hey, it could even be writing a book. Whatever it is, go out and just start doing it. The world is filled with people who will disapprove of any move you make. Why would you change your major? Why would you start a new business? If you listen to everyone's opinions about what you should do, you will never do anything. Sometimes it is best to let your actions speak for you. You also do not want to be known as the "all talk" person. We all know the friend who talks about doing this and that. Yet, they never end up doing it. They will start a business, yet when you ask how it is coming along, they just say that it was too difficult and gave up. If you just put your head down and grind away at your dreams, people will see. They do not need to hear about it; they will see it when you have it completed. If you are not satisfied with what you are doing, what makes you think others will? No validation is better than internal validations. When you are happy with your philosophies, then others will be too.

October 10th

"He who is not every day conquering some fear has not learned the secret of life."

- Ralph Waldo Emerson: 19th Century American Philosopher

In order to conquer some fear, it must mean that you take on the responsibility of overcoming a fearsome situation. There are many different fears that you may come across when you get to college. You might be pretty scared because this is your first time on your own and have never had to do your own laundry. How do you conquer the small fear of doing your own laundry for the first time? There are many ways to overcome this fear. The first is trial-and-error. Put your clothes in the washer and set it to cold and see how everything comes out. You will eventually find the right way to wash all your clothes. You can look up "how to wash your clothes" on the internet and watch some videos. You can even ask someone in the laundry room for help and use the excuse you are not familiar with that type of washer and dryer. You will pick up some real problem-solving skills as you go about conquering your fears. Conquering your fears allows for you to grow as a person. Now you can do your laundry and conquer any fear that comes your way.

October 11th

"Stay calm and serene regardless of what life throws at you."

- Marcus Aurelius: Roman Emperor & Stoic Philosopher

Life sometimes sucks. There are days when life throws everything at you, and you just have to go with it. There are weeks when college decides to put all your exams and paper due dates on the same week, and you just have to do it. Your work and social schedule will probably intersect, and you will have to miss out on activities with friends and family. No one said that every day will be sunshine and rainbows when you go off to college. There are days where it sucks. The best thing you can do these days is take a deep breath and just roll with the punches. You cannot really fight these things, because you do not have much power. Go with the flow and try your best to do everything you have to do. Sure, it is not fun, but if you react to these things with anger, disapproval, and annoyance, you are just making it harder on yourself. Go into these situations with a calm mind that will allow you to figure out the best plan of attack and then do it.

October 12th

"A horse never runs so fast as when he has other horses to catch up and outpace."

- Ovid: Ancient Roman Poet

Winning is not everything. This is a saying that you have heard before in life, probably when you lost something. It is normal to not win at everything you do. No one is great at everything they do. Winning is not everything, but do not let that saying allow you to accept mediocrity. Sure, you might not be the best at something, but that does not mean you are just going to settle there. You can always work and get better at whatever you are doing. You will not get A's on all your tests, but that does not mean you should try not to get A's. You will not be the best public speaker, but that does not mean you do not try to be better. It is one thing to not win because you were not the best; it is another thing to not try to win. You should have a little competitive spirit in you. You are going to win a lot more if you try to win rather than settle for "winning is not everything."

October 13th

"The wisest men follow their own direction."
- Euripides: Ancient Greek Tragedian

We often fall victim to falling in line with others. You will just do what everyone else is doing because you do not want to be different. There is a bad stigma around being different. It should not be wrong to do things different than someone else. However, we often look down on people who do not follow the group or may do something different from everyone else. You do not always need to do something the same way as everyone else; it is okay to be different. If you have a dream that requires you to take a different life path than everyone else, you should not feel bad for taking that path; embrace that it is unique and feel good about it. Think of how impossible civilization would be if every human being did the exact same thing. Your path might not be the same as all your friends, but it is the path you need to take. If you are worried about your friends thinking less of you, you need to realize that they will support you if they are really your friends. You are a unique being, and you have a unique path in life. Follow that path even if it is different from everyone else's.

October 14th

"It is not what you endure, but how you endure it that matters."

- Lucius Annaeus Seneca: Roman Stoic Philosopher

We all have our own struggles that we have to bear. Some people have more than others, but everyone has to endure something. In college, you are around so many different people from all walks of life. Each of them has various issues that they have to overcome. Some people will run from their problems; others will suppress them. Not only do these ways not help you brave through your struggles, but they only make your problems worse. It is really sad to see someone throw their life away because they could not endure what needed to be taken. You can use excuses for the issues you have to endure, but excuses are not going to make these issues go away. The best way is to face your problems head-on and endure whatever is thrown at you. It does not matter how much you have to fight to get through these issues; no one can blame you for fighting. Once you have finally figured out how to overcome your struggles, you can look back and realize that it did not matter how you did it, rather you just did it.

October 15th

"Even from a foe a man may learn wisdom."
- *Greek Proverb*

A hard lesson in life is that not everyone will like you. You are also not going to like everyone that you meet. You will probably tend to avoid people that you do not like. If you end up crossing paths with someone you do not like, this does not mean that you need to be rude to them. You cannot like someone but treat them well and even learn something from them. Everyone has some wisdom that can be instilled upon you, even people you do not like. The knowledge they give you might actually change your perspective on them and your relationship with them. Typically, you do not like people who do not like you. They will tell you things about yourself without sugarcoating it like your friends would. If your haircut looks bad, they will tell you and not excuse it like your friends did. If they do not agree with your thoughts, they let you know. There is no easing into it. You do not have to like everyone, but you can still learn a thing or two from them.

October 16th

"Use your fear; it can take you to the place where you store your courage."

- Amelia Earhart: 20th Century Aviator

Not only is college one of the most exciting and fun times, but it can also be one of the most terrifying times in your life. The reason that it can be pretty scary is that there is so much unknown. This is probably one of the first times you are on your own; you do not have parents and teachers constantly looking after you. You are also perhaps in a new town with many new people. Being in a new place with many people you do not know can be scary. Then you throw in college and the amount of coursework you will have to do. So, if you feel any of these fears, what do you do? Yes, college is a big place, and there are many people. Use that fear to gain the courage to explore and make some friends. Use that courage to go to your classes and do well. The good thing about this is the sooner you get the courage, everything stops being so scary. Everyone gets a bit scared or nervous about all the unknowns in college. Use that feeling to muster up some courage and face those fears, and before you know it, you will not be scared of it anymore.

October 17th

"When we are in love we seem to ourselves quite different from what we were before."

- Blaise Pascal: 17th Century French Philosopher & Theologian

---

We may not realize it, but we are usually pretty hard on ourselves. We often struggle to find good qualities about ourselves. This all changes when we fall in love. It is probably because someone else sees your qualities and enjoys them too. You start to think that maybe you are just too hard on yourself. If someone else can like these qualities about you, then you probably should too. This makes you realize that we should all love ourselves a little more; learn to have some self-love. This is a pretty important concept because if you think about it, why should anyone love you if you cannot even love yourself? This is not sending a great message out to others. People like to see someone with some confidence and love for themselves. We all have some pretty good qualities that we exhibit. You probably are overthinking how bad these qualities are. More than likely other people do not think they are that bad. We see ourselves differently when in love, so start loving yourself.

October 18th

"To live happily is an inward power of the soul."
- Marcus Aurelius: Roman Emperor & Stoic Philosopher

No one wants to live a miserable life. We all feel the best and do the best for others when we are happy. One way to become happy is to chase after things that we desire. It could be some new clothes, a new phone, or even your favorite meal. These things bring us happiness temporarily, however. The pleasure we feel from material goods is nice for a little bit but soon wears off. When material objects are no longer bringing you true happiness, you have the choice to look inwardly for happiness. True happiness can be found when you look inside. Is your soul upset, and you mask that feeling with material goods to help you feel better? You are never going to be truly happy, unless your soul is happy. Look and see what it is that your soul is feeling. Find nonmaterial things to help the soul become happy. Maybe your soul is darkened because it lacks purpose. Find something that you are good at and brings you pleasure. Perhaps it is searching for meaning, in which case you can turn to religion. When you can create a content soul, you will live a content life.

October 19th

"There is no shame in not knowing; the shame lies in not finding out."

- Russian Proverb

Let us think about this example: You sit in class while the professor is lecturing over a concept that you do not understand. You do not want to look stupid for asking a question, so you do not ask. The weeks go by, and finally, it is test week. There are several questions on the test about that concept you went over in class. You have no idea how to do any of those problems, and thus you do pretty badly on the test. Think about which you would rather have: a moment of dumbness or a test grade that proves it. There is nothing wrong with asking a question. There really are no dumb questions. Sure, you might have the attention drawn to you for a few moments, but if you gain a better understanding of your question, was it not worth it? The problem of not asking questions lies in the future when you are tested on those concepts that you do not understand. There is no shame in asking questions in college; the only time when you should feel justified shame is when you get that test back with a bad score on it, and it could have all been fixed if you just would have asked that question.

October 20th

"The greater the difficulty, the more the glory in surmounting it."

- Epicurus: Ancient Greek Philosopher

It is hard to look at that big exam you have coming up and feel excited about it. You are already thinking about the hours you will spend studying for this exam. Or maybe you already get nervous about being in the testing room, and you are completely blanking on all the material for this test. There is no way around it. This is going to be a difficult exam. However, the more difficult the exam, the better you will feel once you complete it. Think of the relief you will feel when you submit that exam. Now think about how good you will feel when you see that you passed it. All of that work and stress that you experienced for this now feels worth it. You will have big tests all your life, even after you leave school. Sure, we can be nervous and scared for them, but just remember that the bigger the test, the greater the feeling of accomplishment you will get for completing it. If you can rise to the challenge, the rewarding feelings afterward will make it all worth it.

October 21st

"Prosperity comes through vigilance, energy, and wise counsel."

― Roman Proverb

We all want to have prosperity in whatever we do, whether it be a job, a family, or anything else. A few pointers can help you obtain prosperity a bit easier. One of them is vigilance. You are bound to encounter some bad in your life, but if you are vigilant toward it, you will not suffer as much as if you were blindsided by it. It is a lot easier to recover from something bad if you know it before it happens. Keep vigilant, and nothing will throw you off. Prosperity is also going to require some work. It will not be easy, and the road to it will be hard. You have to maintain energy in your quest for prosperity. Without any energy or drive, you will never accomplish what you want. You have a memory for a reason; remember experiences, hold knowledge from the past and apply it to the future. Use what you know and learn from your past mistakes to do better in the future. You cannot have prosperity if you continuously make mistakes over the same problem. Use these three pieces of advice to get you started, and you will be on the road to prosperity.

October 22nd

"Devote the rest of your life to making progress."
- Epictetus: Ancient Greek Philosopher

Do you think you deserve an A on that test you received a C on? Or maybe you believe you deserve to be in a better relationship with your partner. What are you going to do to get what you deserve? You will have to work every day to become better at what you want until you get it. Maybe that requires staying in a few more nights a week to study rather than going out. Or perhaps it means dumping your toxic partner and getting with someone who respects you. If you truly want to make progress, you will need to make some changes. You do not need to make huge steps in progress every single day. Still, if you work little by little every day, you will make some serious progress toward whatever goal you have in mind. This discipline will help you even after you graduate college. It does not matter what you do, as long as you do it with discipline, you will see great success. Trust the process, and you will get to the end goal before you even know it.

October 23rd

"Don't neglect the future in times of plenty, for tomorrow you may need what you wasted today."

- Aesop: Ancient Greek Fabulist

You are in arguably the greatest part of your life. You are young, healthy, and pretty happy. You are no longer young enough to need your parents' permission to do stuff and not old enough yet to have a spouse and kids and other family obligations. Life is great now, but any person over the age of forty will tell you that it slowly starts getting more difficult. You can be an idiot and party and drink all you want now because it has little to no effect on you. You can be in as many relationships as you want now, because you are young, and time is on your side. What you should not do is neglect your future just because times are good now. You do not want to be a thirty-five-year-old person still going to frat parties. You do not want to be single and in and out of relationships for the rest of your life. This is not to say do not enjoy yourself, you absolutely can. Just make sure you are aware that your college years will end, and you need to be sure you did not waste too much of your potential away.

October 24th

"When you doubt your power, you give power to your doubt."

- Honoré De Balzac: 19th Century French Novelist & Playwright

---

When incoming college students begin their new journey, they realize that this might not be the college experience like you see in the movies. This can lead to many college students' minds racing with thoughts of doubt. You might be doubtful if you chose the right major to study, or the best friends to hang out with, or the right school. The good news is that all college students experience these thoughts of doubt at least once in their lives. When you fill your mind with doubt, you are only giving power to these bad thoughts. You cannot overthink your doubtful thoughts. College is a time for you to mess up and fail. It might mean that you switch majors or that you find out your dream school was not the right school for you. Do not let these doubtful thoughts control you. Rather than giving doubt power, try doing some things to eliminate those doubtful thoughts. One way is to surround yourself with supportive people who encourage you and give you a helpful boost of confidence. Do not let doubt limit you from the great things you will do in college.

October 25th

"No one is so brave that he is not disturbed by something unexpected."

- *Julius Caesar: Roman General & Statesman*

If your professors are nice, they will give you a semester schedule of assignments, tests, quizzes, and everything else you might have due. This takes a lot of stress off of you, so you are not left in the dark about when things will happen. Sometimes it is nice to plan out everything in your life, so there are no surprises. Everything is neatly in order. Yes, that sounds nice, but is that really what you want? Having everything planned out in your life, leaving nothing up to chance. Do not be upset when events and problems pop up unexpectedly. This is what makes life, well, life. It adds a little bit of interest to the mundane of our planned lives. When they happen, they really screw up your schedule, and it causes some stress, but sometimes that is what you need in life. You can always take the attitude that it is something new that you get to experience, so you might as well make the most of it. Enjoy the unexpected things in life. They are what makes it interesting.

October 26th

"This above all; to thine own self be true."
- William Shakespeare: 16th Century English Playwright & Poet

---

Are you doing this because you want to, or because everyone around you is doing it? You have gone through most of your life doing the same things as everyone else around you. You went to school, took the same classes, played the same sports, and did the same activities as your peers. You leave for college, and you are no longer forced to be part of what everyone else does. You now have the freedom to be your own person. This can lead you to question, what does it mean to be you? To find this out, you have to look inside. If you never stop and look inside, you will go through life never being your true self. You can have things you want to do and accomplish in life, but until you look inside to see your desires, you will never know for sure what your dreams really are. When you find that vision inside yourself, you will have a newfound purpose in life, almost like you have become a new person. Look inside and find your vision, and then go begin working on it.

October 27th

"It's too late to shut the stable door after the horse has bolted."

- Norwegian Proverb

There are times when you cannot prevent something from happening, and there are times when you can. The things that you can control, you should try to control. You can manage your temper and how you react to situations and people. You totally determine it, and you should learn how to handle that. There are also things in life that you cannot control. These are usually the awful things of life, but you cannot do anything about them. You cannot control if it will rain today, or if the traffic is going to be bad. You also cannot control if someone falls out of love with you. These things will happen, and some of them can leave you pretty upset. This is when you just have to accept the situation for what it is and learn your lesson; there is not much you can do in these types of problems. You will learn to conquer those things in your control and be at peace with those things outside of it. Sometimes the horses bolt loose, and there is nothing you can do. There is no point in shutting the door if they are gone. All you can do is move on and do better next time.

October 28th

"Every new beginning comes from some other beginning's end."

- Lucius Annaeus Seneca: Roman Stoic Philosopher

It can be hard not to think about people we dislike. They obviously did something that was upsetting to you, and that anger over the person is manifesting inside of you. Why would you think about them if this is what they are doing to you? You are causing nothing but pain and suffering to yourself thinking about this person. Sure, that person hurt you, but do you think they deserve to be thought about? If they really hurt you as badly as what you feel, then they should be completely out of your life, including inside your head. There is no reason to feel this pain every second of the day, so stop thinking about them. It is obviously easier said than done. Start distracting yourself with stuff that you like. Pick up some old hobbies you dropped, start playing video games or reading, literally anything. If you divert your mind to something you are doing, it does not have time to start thinking about another person. Happy thoughts make for a happy life. Eliminate the bad ones, and let the good ones in.

October 29th

"Blame yourself as you blame others; forgive others as you forgive yourself."

- Chinese Proverb

Usually, when we blame other people, we are not easy on them. Someone else is told to do something that needs to be done, and when they do not do this, we see that as a complete failure. It also does not help that when most people fail, it affects us. On the flip side, we often quickly write it off as not a big deal when we mess up. We do not think our one mistake is the end of the world. You need to start holding yourself to the same standard as others. Think about how upset you would be if someone did to you what you did to them. Likewise, you also need to learn how to forgive. Forgiveness is the best way to totally move on from a situation. We are often quick to forgive ourselves because we do not often think we are the problem. It is important to sympathize with others and put yourself in their shoes. You should show them the same forgiveness that you offer yourself. Hold yourself to a higher standard and understand what others are going through.

October 30th

"My course is set for an uncharted sea."
- Dante Alighieri: 13th Century Italian Poet & Writer

◆

Obviously, you have some big dreams since you are off to college or already in college. Getting a degree and then getting the job you have always wanted is what several of your peers are dreaming of. Maybe you were not the best student in high school and did not make the best grades, but do not let that deter you from your dreams. No one situation can define you. You will have a tougher path than some others, but that will only make the end more worth it. You are going to stumble and fall on your climb to your dreams. These are the times when you will wonder if this dream of yours is actually worth it. Keep sailing, and do not let these moments of failure keep you from your ultimate goal. Sometimes it will feel like a long shot, and loss seems more likely than success. Usually, it is the darkest right before the sun comes up, so be ready to take some risks for your dream. Those risks and stumbles will make reaching the top so worth it.

October 31st

"What the superior man seeks is in himself; what the smaller man seeks is in others."
- *Confucius: Ancient Chinese Philosopher*

You have felt the pain of doing less than you are capable of. When you take a test feeling that you did pretty well, and then you get the test back and bombed it. This is upsetting because you know what you can do, and you fell short of that. In the aspect of life, that was one little test. However, a memory similar to that example probably popped into your mind. Now, imagine that you did less than you were capable of in life. Not just a test, not a class, not a job, but your life. You have a standard inside you that you know when you are doing as good as you can. This standard will lead you to all that you have ever wanted in life. That feeling that you felt after you got that test back, imagine feeling that every single day. If you do not wish that empty feeling inside of you every day, you should start acting on everything in your life with all the capability that you can. You can look back and think that you gave it your everything on all you did. That is something to be happy about.

November

November 1st

"Great things are done by a series of small things brought together."

- Vincent Van Gogh: 19th Century Dutch Painter

Completing college is no small feat. It can seem pretty daunting as a freshman just first starting to believe you can make this goal possible. When you look at college as a large task, it is brutally daunting. However, you can break it down into tiny tasks that when put together make up the big picture of getting a college degree. Find the smallest way to break it down that you feel you can obtain. You can break it down semester by semester, and even smaller by doing week by week. Each week you complete is a tiny puzzle piece being added to the puzzle. Each semester you complete is a small fragment of the puzzle starting to fit together. As you complete your weeks and semesters, pretty soon you are going to have a completed puzzle. This is much easier than trying to put the puzzle together all at once. When you have any project ahead of you that seems pretty difficult to complete, always try to break it down into smaller, more manageable pieces. If you manage to bring enough small pieces together, then you will build something great.

November 2nd

"Wherever there is a human being, there is an opportunity for a kindness."

- Lucius Annaeus Seneca: Roman Stoic Philosopher

◆

Our actions are often based on a "what is in it for me" type of process. We will do something for someone, as long as there is some benefit for you in it. This is typical; we are all somewhat selfish by nature. Why would you want to do something that requires time and energy if you walk away from it empty-handed? Sometimes, it is not bad that you are left empty-handed. Giving and helping others does not always have to benefit you. If you can show an act of kindness to someone else with no expectation of a reward, then at some point, that same act will be given to you. It is sort of like paying it forward. It should bring you some peace, knowing that if you can do something so selflessly, there is probably someone else who could do the same for you. Not everything you do requires that you get rewarded for it. Sometimes, it is best to just act out of your goodness as a person. If the roles were reversed, you would hope for the same from someone else.

November 3rd

"To the wise, life is a problem; to a fool, a solution."
- Marcus Aurelius: Roman Emperor & Stoic Philosopher

Problems are a part of our lives and are far from escapable. It is impossible to get through college without encountering a single problem along the way. Being able to overcome problems is what living is really about. It gives us meaning. This meaning comes from growing as a person; we must endure and learn from problems in our lives. Too many people try to avoid their problems because they are uncomfortable, but this distress is where we grow. When you have academic obstacles, you will figure out how to become the best student you can be. You will find out about yourself when you work through personal issues. You can avoid your problems for a while, but they will inevitably catch up to you. In order to live a better life, you must learn how to overcome your problems. Do not fear the problems that arise in your life; rather, accept them as they are and rise to the challenge of overcoming them. This is a better way to live than a perfectly problem-free life.

November 4th

"The road to success is dotted with many tempting parking spaces."

- Will Rogers: 20th Century American Actor

Along your road to success, you will notice several spots where you could just stop and be fine. Maybe your goal is to graduate and get a master's degree. Along the way, you will notice that you could stop going to college after you complete enough credits for an associate degree. You could make a decent living and live a good life with that. However, this is not your goal. You may also notice that you could stop at getting a bachelor's degree. You would make an even better living and have a good life. However, this is not the goal you set for yourself. There are always places to stop on the road to your personal successes, but if you really want to get to that finish line, you cannot stop. Those options may seem nice now, but wait until the future when you look back with regret for not continuing on. You do not want to live with the regret of not continuing on your path because you were tired or had thoughts of giving up. Yes, there will be times when you are tired, and it feels impossible. As long as you keep going, you will be at that finish line before you know it.

November 5th

"Trust thyself: every heart vibrates to that iron string."
- Ralph Waldo Emerson: 19th Century American Philosopher

You may not have been a great student coming out of high school. You might not be the best or most talented person to graduate in your class. Lucky for you, college is basically a fresh start. You can change everything you felt you did wrong in high school and become a better you. We all have the potential to do great things; it is just that some of us never tap into that potential and use it to go anywhere. The potential for you to do something amazing is there. You just have to use it. Self-confidence is another thing you can reinvent about yourself. Maybe you did not do the best in high school. Now you are starting over, so you have the chance to become a better student. This should give you a boost in confidence. You can start off as a confident student. After all, you have no reason to feel bad about your college studies, because you have never been to college before! You can change a lot in this world. The key to doing so is to find your inner potential and use it and have some confidence in yourself.

November 6th

"To understand the true quality of people, you must look into their minds, and examine their pursuits and aversions."

- Marcus Aurelius: Roman Emperor & Stoic Philosopher

It does not take a scientist to figure out which people aspire for greatness and which ones just settle. Look and see what the person is doing with their life. Are they partying every night and on the verge of academic probation, or are they studying to become a better student? Do they have a sense of purpose, or are they just going through the motions of life? A person who has no goals or aspirations in life will not have the qualities you want to surround yourself with. The same process can be used on yourself. Look inside yourself and figure out if you have goals to propel yourself forward. If you are avoiding something that will make you a better person, you are allowing yourself to settle for less than you are capable. Take a moment to look around at what you and everyone around you are doing. Actions speak louder than words. Doing this will show you the true quality of your life and the quality of others' lives that surround you.

November 7th

"Whoever is happy will make others happy too."
- Anne Frank: 20th Century German Diarist

Life just feels better when you are in a good mood. There will be days when it feels like college life gives you a bad perspective. Whether it is homework, exams or roommate issues, there are just days when you will not be happy. It is okay to not have good days. You just have to ensure that those bad days do not turn into bad stretches. Having a bad day is fine; heck, even a bad few days is acceptable. When it starts turning into bad weeks and months, you need to do something about that. It is no fun to constantly be miserable, so why not go fix the issue? Confront your roommates about the issue or talk to your professor about that test. Because once you get the problems sorted out, you can start to move on to a happier life. Plus, when you are happy, then everyone around you is too. Your roommates are not avoiding you, and your professors will be pleased that they helped you out. Try to see the good of every day and enjoy life. Being happy is a choice, and it is probably the best choice you can make.

November 8th

"Our greatest weakness lies in giving up. The most certain way to succeed is always to try just one more time."
- Thomas Edison 19th Century American Inventor

People are always so confused about how to obtain success. Authors will make whole careers of writing series about how to be successful. Here is how you can find success in one short page. You need to have a plan to have success. If you start working toward a goal with no plan, you will encounter issues and have no idea what to do. So, get a plan, and then start to work. Using your plan as a guide, start working hard at whatever you need to do to make that dream a reality. This next part is where many people stop. They encounter failure and see that as a reason to give up. Instead of giving up, they should look at loss as a learning opportunity. You messed up, and now you have learned to not mess up like that again. Do not consider it a failure, but more like gaining knowledge through error. If you can stick to your plan, work hard at your craft every day, and learn from your failures, then you will have success in whatever you choose.

November 9th

"Speaking without thought is like shooting without taking aim."

- *Spanish Proverb*

Before you speak, think about what you are revealing to everyone with your words. The language you use toward others shows them the type of person you are. The way you talk and what you say sticks with people. If you do not think before you speak when you are mad at someone, you will let your emotions get the better of you. You scream at the other person, and it shows them who you really are. You may be able to present yourself well to others with how you dress or how you look, but the moment you speak, you show others who you are inside. That person might forgive you for yelling at them, but they will never forget what you said. Now you are known by the unkind way you speak. You will be judged by what you say to others, so make sure that you are being judged favorably with the things you say. If you speak kindly to others, you will be remembered as a kind person. Thinking before you speak will allow you to decide if opening your mouth will benefit others and your own reputation, or if it might be better to stay quiet.

November 10th

"What is not started today is never finished tomorrow."
- *Johann Wolfgang Von Goethe: 18th Century German Poet & Playwright*

Many of us played with Legos as kids. Whether you were a fan of building them or not, you at least know what the concept of Legos is. When you played with them, you started with some bigger pieces and connected them together. You then began to stack one piece on top of the other. You then joined two larger sets of pieces together. Pretty soon, you had this giant work of Lego art. You can also think of this as a metaphor for life. What are you trying to accomplish, and how are you building up to that accomplishment? It starts with a single piece, and you have to connect that to another piece. You connect one piece of your dream to another piece. You keep building and connecting until you are satisfied with your work. Sometimes the pieces fall apart; that happens in life too. You just have to put the pieces back together and keep building. Just like your Lego masterpiece, it will require some time to build your dream, but when you finish, you are going to be proud of what you made. Your goals do not come prebuilt; you have to put them together yourself.

November 11th

"Happiness is a journey, not a destination."
- Buddha: Ancient Indian Religious Leader

You have been going to college for awhile now, and you are stressed out. It was not all parties and fun like you thought it might be the first few weeks. All your classes are drowning you in homework, reading, and tests. You are overwhelmed and stressed out. These feelings often lead to anger or sadness. You are angry that everything is not going as smoothly as you wanted, or you are sad that everything feels like it is crumbling around you. This is not the college experience you thought it was going to be. You need to change something, or you are going to go crazy. Well, you need to start being happy. It may seem now like you have a lot to do, but if you do nothing but work all the time, you actually might go crazy. Take a few hours to relax and do something that you find enjoyable. Go out with friends or lay in bed and watch a movie. One of the main purposes in life is to enjoy it, and if you are doing nothing enjoyable, you will not be happy. Take some time to keep your spirits up and do the things you enjoy; it makes the work you have to do a little less awful.

November 12th

"It is not that we have a short time to live, but that we waste much of it."
- Lucius Annaeus Seneca: Roman Stoic Philosopher

You might be looking at all that you need to accomplish in the next week and think it is impossible. The number of papers, assignments, and tests seems insurmountable for one person. You feel that you do not have enough time in a day to complete what you need to get done. Well, stop and think about how much of a day you waste, and think about how you could use that time toward what you need to get done. If you do not wake up until one in the afternoon and look at your phone for the next few hours, it is no surprise that you feel you do not have enough time in your day to get stuff done. If you were to wake up at ten in the morning, rather than one in the afternoon, and focus on your work before looking at your phone, that is a solid five extra hours you now have to complete your weeks worth of work. The amount of work that you had to accomplish seems much more manageable when you are not wasting your time on other less important things. You could get so much more accomplished if you spent your time working on your tasks at hand rather than wasting it away.

November 13th

"Do the difficult things while they are easy and do the great things while they are small. A journey of a thousand miles must begin with a single step."
- Lao Tzu: Ancient Chinese Philosopher

How do you start doing something you have never done before? Well, as simple as it sounds, you just start. When you go to college, you will not be given a step-by-step guide to everything you have to do. You just do it the first time and go from there. This is how you will go about chasing everything in your life. You take that first step and start walking. You will figure out college as you go along. Figuring out how college works will never happen if you do not take that first step. Sure, it is hard sometimes to take that first step if you have no idea what you are getting yourself into. Think about those goals that you have. Are you going to wait in fear to take those first steps, or just start walking? Failure and setbacks are going to happen. You cannot let those stop you from starting. You will learn from those failures, and you will try again and again until you succeed. Set aside your fears and take that first step toward your goals and dreams. You will not regret it.

November 14th

"A man should be upright, not be kept upright."
- Marcus Aurelius: Roman Emperor & Stoic Philosopher

Growing up, you always had people around you who made sure that you were doing what you needed to. You parents made sure that you did your chores and homework in their home. Your teachers made sure that you were doing your schoolwork and staying out of trouble during the school day. These people have made sure that you stay on the right path as best they can. Now that you have moved off to college, you do not have anybody looking out for you to make sure you do what you have to do. You are now fully in charge of yourself. Living on your own means that your parents are not there to check if you have done your homework or not. Your professors are not going to be concerned if you do not show up to class. You now have to be self-supporting. This means that you have to be mature enough to not suffer from this new freedom of not being checked on. You now have to keep yourself going on your own. This can be difficult at first for many college students, but the more you practice this self-sufficiency, the better you will get.

November 15th

"Victory comes from finding opportunities in problems."
- Sun Tzu: Ancient Chinese Military Strategist & Philosopher

You have countless opportunities ahead of you in these next few years. The biggest one is that you have the chance to start becoming whatever you want. Never before have you been able to say, "I want to become x," and you get to start learning about how to become x. You will have the opportunity to get internships, academic awards, and scholarships. You might think to yourself that these will come to you by chance, that you will get lucky, and one of these things will fall into your lap. However, this is not how opportunity works. Opportunity only comes around when you work to create a path for it to come to you. You will get academic awards if you study and work really hard in your classes. If you do none of these things, then the opportunity for an academic award will likely miss you. The same can be said for internships and scholarships as well. You have to put yourself in the path of opportunity. Go and work to that goal, and if you keep working hard enough, an opportunity will find you.

November 16th

"Never let the fear of striking out keep you from playing the game."

- Babe Ruth: 20th Century American Baseball Player

Do we all have something we fear? Absolutely. Are there things you are going to be scared of at college? Probably. Maybe you have never been in a classroom of more than twenty people, and your first class in college has a hundred. Or perhaps you are not the best at talking to groups of people, and you are enrolled in a public speaking class. There will be times in college when you will be pushed out of your comfort zone. This is totally okay, as long as you look at it as an opportunity to learn and grow. Sure, there are some things in college you may not like as much, but do not let that be the reason you stop going to college. Some classes are going to challenge you, but do not let your fear stop you from taking those classes. This class might be challenging and push you out of your comfort zone, but this is good for you because it allows you to learn how to deal with adversity. You end up learning more in the classes that really challenge you. Do not run away from these fears, but embrace the challenge and face them.

November 17th

"Turn your face towards the sun and the shadows fall behind you."

- Maori Proverb

When nothing in your life seems to go right, it is easy to fall into the darkness of it. Whatever you are going through, if all you think about and surround yourself with is pain, you will be trapped in the darkness of that pain. To get out of the dark, you should go to the light. Try to find something good in your life and focus your attention on that. Looking toward the light, turn your back to the dark. If you are heartbroken, and all you do is surround yourself with pictures of you two and sad music, then you are just immersing yourself in pain and hurt. Throw the images away, go out with your friends, and do something you like doing. Those fun activities and being with friends take your mind away from the pain you feel. When you do activities that you enjoy and spend time with people you like, it turns your back to the pain for a moment. Putting the bad behind you and moving forward is the first step to finding peace again. So do not let yourself stay in the dark; rather, do what makes you happy and turn your back on the darkness and let the light shine on you.

November 18th

"To know what people really think, pay regard to what they do rather than what they say."

- Rene Descartes: 17th Century French Philosopher

It is easy to accept what people say just because they said it. We have all experienced this problem before. People think they will do something for you but never do it. Sure, they said they would, but they never acted on it. Basically, it was just a bunch of empty words. It is much easier to believe someone based on their actions than on their statements. Being able to lead by action rather than by words makes it much more believable to everyone else what your intentions are. If you want sincerity in your life, do not just say it; there needs to be an action that follows. Act as an honest person, and everyone around you can see that they are not just empty words but real action that you exhibit. If you want honesty from another person, do not just let them say that they want it; they have to act on it. If they cannot work on it, then it is probably true that they do not believe it either. If you really want to know what a person has intentions for, do not listen to their words but look at their actions.

November 19th

"The object of life is not to be on the side of the majority, but to escape finding oneself in the ranks of the insane."

- Marcus Aurelius: Roman Emperor & Stoic Philosopher

You do not want to go through college conforming to the masses with every decision you make. This is a hard concept to fully grasp because you do not want to be the only person who is not part of the group. You are finally on your own with the capacity to make your own decisions, so take advantage of it! Sure, there are times when it is good to be a part of the majority at college. Being a fan of the school's athletics is something that most people would be on the same side for. What you should do is try to evaluate if it is wise to be a part of the majority if it means being just like everyone else. Look into the ideas and ideologies of the majority, and determine if it would be something you would join in on. Would you join it if there was no big crowd? If you would not conform to these ideas if there was no majority, then it means that it still will not be a good idea with a majority. You are independent now, so enjoy that and do your own thing.

November 20th

"Where you go, go with all your heart."
- Confucius: Ancient Chinese Philosopher

Whatever you do, go all out on it. There is never a reason to doing something halfway. Why would you only complete half of a test or only show up willing to give half effort? Just think of how bad some things can end if you give less than everything. You might think that the term "half-hearted" refers to only your effort. Teachers and coaches often use this expression to let you know that you are not giving the best effort that you can. In reality, "half-hearted" can be for just about anything—energy, motivation, participation, discipline, enthusiasm, etc. There is almost no end to things that you can do half-heartedly. This also means that there is no end to something that you can do with your heart. Be enthusiastic and fully motivated to do what you want to do. If you are not willing to do something full-heartedly, there is no real reason to even do it. Do whatever you want full-heartedly in every aspect that you can think of. The outcomes will always be better than if you gave just half of it.

November 21st

"Don't judge each day by the harvest you reap but by the seeds that you plant."

- Robert Louis Stevenson: 19th Century Scottish Novelist & Poet

---

It is easy to see your progress when you are rewarded for it. When you get good grades, you judge that you are doing pretty well. When you are starting your dream business, it is easy to tell yourself that you are doing good when making lots of sales. But what are you going to do when the successes are not rolling in? It can feel like you have failed because you have not seen any success. You may not be getting constant recognition for what you are doing, but as long as you put in the work, you are making progress. Do not get discouraged when the rewards do not show up, because this does not mean you are doing badly. It just means that the success is not there yet. All of that studying might not feel worth it right now, but when you do well on that test in a few weeks, you will feel better. Putting in the small work on your side business will eventually get you the recognition you want. Good things take time, and your success is no different. Do not be upset because nothing successful happened today. Just remember you made steps in the right direction.

November 22nd

"By committing foolish acts, one learns wisdom."
— *Singhalese Proverb*

You know what it is like to be the idiot in the room. We have all been there before when we do something or say something stupid, and everyone is laughing at us. It is not always the best feeling in the world, but it is actually a great learning point in your life. There are only a few ways to learn how to do something, and failure is one. You will look stupid when you fail, but this is a key point in the learning process. As weird as it sounds, it is actually good to look stupid every once in a while. You learn about the situation and a better way to do it again in these moments. If you mess up giving a speech, you will learn from those mistakes and will be able to move forward to becoming a great public speaker. Looking like an idiot will not be the most enjoyable feeling ever, but it will pass. You might remember it for a while because it was pretty traumatic for you, but because it was just a funny moment to others, it will be out of their heads in a few days. So do not beat yourself up for making mistakes and looking like a fool, because this is one of the best ways to learn and become wiser.

November 23rd

"It is not only what we do, but also what we do not do, for which we are accountable."

- Moliere: 17th Century French Playwright

Accountability means you are responsible for your actions. You are responsible for the actions that you have carried out. Other times those actions are things that you did not do but should have. There are many examples of things you should do but do not. You did not go to class today because you did not feel like it, but you should have. You should write that paper, but you did not because you procrastinated it. You have a test tomorrow and you stayed up all night playing video games when you should have gone to bed. You are accountable for all these things that you did not do. You have not given yourself enough perspective to see the consequences of not doing an action. It is hard to think about the consequences of the actions we do not take, but they often need to be considered. Since you are on your own in college, all decisions fall on you. If you do not want to deal with the backlash of poor decisions, make sure to carefully consider both options of the choice you are accountable for.

November 24th

"He who lives in harmony with himself lives in harmony with the universe."

- Marcus Aurelius: Roman Emperor & Stoic Philosopher

When you are at peace with yourself, the world around you is often peaceful, and likewise when you are not at peace with yourself the world reflects that. What we feel inside is usually directly reflected in what happens around us. When you are in a bad mood, you let your emotions start to dictate what you do. You take your anger out on others, or you sulk around if you feel sad. When you act in this way, the world around you begins to reflect your mood. The people around you become more tense, and you are killing the mood of everyone around you. When you are at peace with yourself, you do not let your emotions dictate what you do. When you have a bad day of class or did not study because the dorm floor was loud, you just brush it off and move on. These events can cause one to become frustrated or sad, which disturbs our inner peace. Find any sort of good in these events, and do not let it bother you that much. When you are good with yourself, you will be good with the world.

November 25th

"It's not because things are difficult that we dare not venture. It's because we dare not venture that they are difficult."

- Lucius Annaeus Seneca: Roman Stoic Philosopher

There are plenty of things that seem scary before you get to college, but once you actually start, they are not so bad. Finding and living with your new roommate can seem pretty scary at first. This complete stranger is who you are going to share a tiny room with. You have probably never met this person before, so you have no idea what type of person you are going to spend your time and space with. Many people will tell you their horror stories about their roommate in college, which may not make you feel much better. Once you get to your dorm or apartment, you will realize that there was nothing to be scared about. Your roommate is just as nervous as you are about the whole college transition. You could become good friends, so everything ends well. Even if you do not like your roommate, there are plenty of other people in your dorm or apartment to get to know and become friends with. You will realize that you were scared about this whole college transition for nothing, and everything turned out great.

November 26th

"Each day provides its own gifts."
- Marcus Aurelius: Roman Emperor & Stoic Philosopher

It is easy to get overwhelmed in college. Once you complete one semester, you really understand how overwhelming it can be. One bit of advice for you is to stop for a moment each day and enjoy the little things that make it special. Too often, we are so occupied with all the big projects and tests that we do not take the time to appreciate the things around us. It does not have to be big things; they can be smaller moments that you may often look past. Perhaps it is the sunrise when you get up to go to class. It could even be as small as experiencing peace and quiet during breakfast or talking on the phone with a family member. Whatever it is, take a moment to realize the gifts you are given each day. Not only does recognizing these gifts put you in a better mood, but it also makes you grateful for what you have. Feeling grateful also makes you feel pretty happy too. Even when you are completely overwhelmed with school, take a moment to realize what a gift it is to study and learn at a college. Each day has its gifts for you; take the time to look and see what they are.

November 27th

"Honesty is the first chapter in the book of wisdom."
- Thomas Jefferson: 3rd President of the United States

We do not like when someone is dishonest with us. You feel like there has been a breach of trust between you and that person. If you do not like when someone else is corrupt with you, why would you want to be dishonest with yourself? Yes, you can lie and be dishonest with yourself. When you lie to yourself, all it does is set you off course to what you really want. Let us say you have a paper that needs to be done this week. You tell yourself that you have plenty of time to do it. This might be truthful at the beginning of the week because you actually do. As the days go by, you continue to tell yourself the same thing. All of a sudden, the paper is due tomorrow. You have been lying to yourself about how much time you have to complete it. All you have done is deceive yourself and set yourself off course. Instead of focusing on finishing this paper when you did have time, you are now struggling to put something together before it is too late. Be honest with yourself and the situations you are in. Honest answers might not always be what you want to hear, but they are what you need.

November 28th

"The breeze at dawn has secrets to tell you."
- Rumi: 13th Century Persian Poet

There are times in life when the best you can do is just get out of bed. We are not superhuman, and there will be days when we are not feeling our best. There will be times when you wake up and are filled with doubts. These doubts could be about anything, but when you let one doubt into your mind, it can begin to let others in too. This can make it very challenging to wake up and be a productive person. It is important to remember that the biggest step you can make in your day is just getting out of your bed. Once you have done this, you have done at least one productive thing. You might not be at your strongest, but if you can get through the day, you have proven to everyone, including yourself, that you are pretty tough. It can take a lot out of you just to do all the required tasks that you have to in a day. Inside your head, you might not be ready for what the world throws at you, but by getting out of bed and walking with your head high, you sure look like you can handle anything.

November 29th

"In anger you should refrain both from speech and action."
- *Pythagoras: Ancient Greek Philosopher*

Anger is a natural human emotion and is totally normal to feel. When you let anger get the better of you, then you look stupid. We have all seen someone's anger get the best of them. They do or say something that they really did not mean, and they make a fool of themselves. We will all be put in situations where anger is bound to pop up inside of us. In these instances, it is just best to take a second to relax or go somewhere else to cool off. When you lose your cool with someone, even if they totally deserve it, you look like an idiot. Not only do you look stupid, but you also will begin to gain a reputation. You do not want to be known as that person who cannot get their anger under control. Do what you need to do to keep your composure and have the discipline to allow yourself to realize you are angry but will not give in to that anger. Nothing good has ever come from talking or acting when your mind is clouded with anger. Chill out, then decide what you need to do.

November 30th

"You may delay, but time will not."
- Benjamin Franklin: 18th Century Writer & Inventor

When you first want to start something, we may ask: "When is a good time to start?" We often ask this question because we do not want to jump into a totally unprepared situation and fail immediately. We would rather wait to start a journey until we are more ready. Unfortunately, you will never be totally prepared for something to happen. You might wonder when the right time to take some of your college classes is. The thought of waiting until next semester will cross your mind. That class will still be new and scary next semester; if you keep thinking like this, you are never going to be ready. Sometimes the best way to get into something is to just jump right in. Yes, this can be scary and stressful, but you have taken the first giant step toward doing it. You might fail, but you also might fail if you waited. There is no "perfect" time to do something, so this should eliminate any fear of you not being ready. Place hope in and enjoy the unknown because it is pretty exciting. You will be glad that you did not wait.

December

December 1st

"Life is neither good or evil, but only a place for good and evil."

- Marcus Aurelius: Roman Emperor & Stoic Philosopher

It sometimes seems like life is not going your way. You scroll through social media and see how great everyone else's life appears to be, while you have multiple exams to study for and will attend a loved one's funeral. There is nothing good about times like these. You might look at the world and think: "Why is my life so bad right now?" Well, your life is not bad; life can be neither good nor bad. The experiences you are experiencing in your life right now are bad, which is not fun. The pain you feel now means you are becoming a well-rounded person from the experience. Soon, your experiences will be good. We have all gone through a period in life when everything that can go right will go right. Sometimes, it will be the exact opposite, and you feel that everything that can go wrong, will. Your life is not inherently awesome or horrible. The experiences you are having now are. Soon, these experiences will be gone, and you will have to face new ones. Do not curse up at the sky asking why your life is bad, because soon it will not be. The good is coming. Just give it a chance.

December 2nd

"Not how long, but how well you have lived is the main thing."

- *Lucius Annaeus Seneca: Roman Stoic Philosopher*

You can think about your life after college. You will go out and have a great career and have a great family. That is all in the future, but someday you will graduate from college and be done with school. When you look back, you want to believe that you did everything you wanted to, with no regrets. You do not want to look back and wish you could do it again because you did not do the things you wanted. So, think about what you want out of your college career, and go out and do it. If you want to look back and think about the great grades you made, then start working at it today. If you go out and start meeting people today, you will look back and think about the great people you met. Go out and try new things. Do not think back and regret not trying something. The last thing you want to do is look back and regret not doing something in college, so go out and do it.

December 3rd

"Some men go through a forest and see no firewood."
                                    - *English Proverb*

It is easy to get tunnel vision when determined to do something. When you are truly focused on something, everything else in the world does not even seem to exist, just you and your goal. While it is good to have determination, it is important to not have tunnel vision so badly that you miss out on opportunities that will help you. It happens to all of us at some point. We are so focused on completing something that we do not even notice the easy solution right before us. You might have a test coming up that you want to do well on, so you will study. You block everything out for a few days to ensure that all you do is study for this class, so you are completely ready. You blocked everything out so much that you did not even notice the professor was holding a study session for the upcoming test. That would have been pretty helpful and seems like a missed opportunity. Being determined is a good thing. Just make sure you do not have the blinders on so high that you miss out on the opportunities in front of you.

December 4th

"He who laughs at himself never runs out of things to laugh at."

- Epictetus: Ancient Greek Philosopher

Think back to yourself in middle school. Pretty rough, right? Not many people can say that their best years were spent in middle school. Looking back, all you can do is laugh at the outfits you wore and the things that you said. Now think back to yourself in high school. There are definitely some moments that you shake your head and wonder why it was that you did those things. What will we think of ourselves now in five years? We are constantly changing and evolving to become the best possible version of ourselves. Looking back and seeing where we are now compared to before, we are different people. You do not even have to think that far back; just think about what you did last week, and you are bound to find something that you cannot believe you did. Whether you want to admit it or not, you do some dumb things sometimes. It is always good to be able to look at yourself and laugh. Being able to laugh at yourself leads to a better and happier life. Because when all else fails, who else are you going to laugh at?

December 5th

"Begin – to begin is half the work, let half still remain; again, begin this, and thou will have finished."

- Marcus Aurelius: Roman Emperor & Stoic Philosopher

Your first real college paper can seem pretty difficult to complete. No longer are teachers asking you to write a two-paragraph paper. You are dealing with multiple-page writing assignments. When you are first handed the rubric and you read your paper needs to be ten to twelve pages, that can be pretty overwhelming. It is easy to put off big papers because they are just too overwhelming. When faced with these big papers, the first and most important thing you can do is to start. Maybe it is reading over the prompt or to start writing an outline. As long as you begin working on the project, you have begun working on it. Beginning a paper is one of the biggest humps to get over, but once you do this, you are committed to getting something done. Now that you have started, you can start figuring out how to get the rest of your tasks complete. Break everything down into manageable and completable tasks, which makes the whole project achievable. Before you know it, you will have that entire paper ready.

December 6th

"When you have exhausted all possibilities, remember this: you haven't."

- Thomas Edison 19th Century American Inventor

Sometimes, it feels like there is no point in getting back up when you get knocked down. You will see people drop a class and switch their major after one bad test grade. They got knocked down and decided to quit. You cannot quit on yourself just because you get knocked down; the only thing that matters is if you get back up. If you fail a test, you will have plenty of other tests to help offset this bad one. You will see people come back from a bad test to end with a really good grade. There are also times when people fail entire courses and come back and still graduate. It does not matter what you failed at, as long as you are willing to get back up and continue marching forward. As you go through college, you will learn to brush off failures and just keep moving. As long as you can keep moving forward, you will accomplish your goals. It is only when you stop and begin to question your failures that you are not likely to keep going. You will complete your goals if you keep getting up after each knockdown.

December 7th

"Let yourself be silently drawn by the strange pull of what you really love. It will not lead you astray."

- Rumi: 13th Century Persian Poet

Sometime after you graduate high school, you will be enrolling for your first semester of college. You will get to look at a course catalog and see all the possible majors and classes. You will have people giving their opinions on what they think you should do. It can be easy to take these opinions to heart and follow what other people say you should do. What these people are telling you are just opinions, nothing else. No one knows yourself as well as you do. You know what your passions are and what your calling really is. Even if you do not see what you want to be, one will draw you more than the other if given a choice between two majors. Before you go to college, it would be a good idea to figure out what your passions are and what you really love to do. Take those passions and find a college degree that best fits those, and that is what you should major in. Do not let others lead you away from your true calling in life. Let what you like draw you to what you want to do.

December 8th

"Take rest; a field that has rested gives a beautiful crop."

- Ovid: Ancient Roman Poet

It can seem like in order to be successful, you always have to be doing something. You may struggle not doing anything because it feels that you should be doing something. Sometimes, taking a well-deserved break is what you really need. Burnout is a real thing, and it is not something that you want to go through. It is good to learn to push through adversity and times when you feel like you should quit. There are only so many times that you can do that. Sometimes, the best thing you can do is take a day to relax and get away from everything. Just lie in bed and watch a few movies, or go for a walk and clear your mind. This gets you recharged and ready to get back to work. It is really hard to accomplish your goals and chase your dreams when you are burnt out. You should never feel bad for taking a day to just rest and recoup from what you have done. If you push through burnout, you are more likely to take less pride in what you are doing and only do it to get it done. If you want to produce the best that you possibly can, you should take a break every once in a while.

December 9th

"What lies behind us and what lies before us are tiny matters compared to what lies within us."
- *Ralph Waldo Emerson: 19th Century American Philosopher*

◆

We all have goals that we want to accomplish and dreams to chase. Every single one of us has a different starting point. Some of you will start with more money, time, experience, or knowledge than others. Just because someone else has more of something than you do, does not mean that your goals are now unobtainable. You just have some extra setbacks you have to work through. We all have different starting points; some start chasing our goals early, while others wait a bit. There is no one way to make a cake; it is the same with making your dreams a reality. Some will obtain them earlier than others, and that is okay. Do not constantly compare how you completed your goals to others. Because in the end, it does not matter. To accomplish your goals, you just need to do what you can do, to the best of your abilities, every single day. Do not worry about things outside your control; just do what you can do. If you do with what you have, you will accomplish your goals and catch your dreams.

December 10th

"The secret of getting things done is to act!"
- Dante Alighieri: 13th Century Italian Poet & Writer

Here is a situation you are all familiar with. You wake up in the morning and feel awful. You might be sick, but not ill enough to stay home. Just sick enough to feel bad all day, or maybe you just had a long night. You roll out of bed and get ready for your day. The motivation to do anything just is not showing up. The only thing you want to do is go plop back into your bed. You have classes and responsibilities that you have to do today. Yet, you do not feel like doing a single thing today. It is a problem of needing to get stuff done with no desire to do anything. We have all been here before. You can do only one thing, so just get started on something. You might not want to do it, but you have to do it. That homework assignment due tonight is not something you are just dying to get started on. If you just sit down and start working on it, it will eventually get done. There is no super secret to being productive when you do not feel like it. You just have to get started working on something, and you will end up having a pretty productive day when you look back on it.

December 11th

"Life is a long lesson in humility."
- James M. Barrie: 20th Century Scottish Novelist & Playwright

---

College will never limit you the number of times you get humbled. You might have been the smartest student in high school, but if you go to a university, you are going to be surrounded by people who are equally if not more intelligent than you. You might have been the best athlete, singer, or musician in high school, but you will find that in any given college classroom, you may no longer be. As unfortunate as this realization can be, it is good to be humbled. Having success immediately with everything you do will only lead to an overinflated ego. Working for something and having success over time is a great way to build humility. When you are humble, you are open to making mistakes and learning from them. You understand the hard work and dedication it takes to obtain success. Being humble also helps those around you. People will be more open and comfortable around you. Just because you are not the best at something now does not mean you will not be eventually; it just means you will be humble about your successes when you get them.

December 12th

"Because a thing seems difficult for you, do not think it impossible for anyone to accomplish."

- *Marcus Aurelius: Roman Emperor & Stoic Philosopher*

You are sitting in class, and you have no idea what you are doing. This class that you are in seems impossible. Now you are wondering if you even belong in this class, let alone college, and feeling like this might just be too much for you. College is no easy feat. Anyone who tells you college is easy is lying. You got to college somehow, so you obviously are good enough to be here. Maybe you do not understand what is happening in your class right now, but you will eventually understand. College will challenge you and force you to think in ways you probably have not before. You are not alone in feeling lost at times. Just know that you are smart enough to get through this, and you will figure it out. Take the time to talk to your professors and work on it outside of class. You will soon forget why you were even stressing over that class.

December 13th

"It is not the man who has little, but the man who craves more, that is poor."

- *Lucius Annaeus Seneca: Roman Stoic Philosopher*

When you step foot on campus, you will come across all kinds of people from all different walks of life. You will see college students around you who have a cooler dorm room or drive a nicer car than you. This can lead you to wanting what others have, which is a slippery slope you may not want to travel. Someone will always have something that is newer or more appealing than what you have. You see someone with the newest model of phone, and it is something you really want. You feel out of place when you look around and you are the only one of your peers with an older model. You want to fit in with everyone else, so you go spent hundreds of dollars on this new phone only for a newer, sleeker phone to be released later. Comparing what you have and do not have with others will only lead you to want more and will always end with you still feeling unhappy. Enjoy what you currently have, because as long as you enjoy it, that is all that really matters. Stop and think about if you really have too little in your life, or are you always wanting too much?

December 14th

"Certain things catch your eye, but pursue only those that capture the heart."

- Ancient Indian Proverb

What is it that captures your heart? In other words, what is it that your heart desires, that you want to have or want to accomplish in life? It is not terribly hard to think of what the heart wants. What do you need to do to obtain those wants and desires? Well, it is going to require some focus. If your heart is set on graduating college, then you will have to focus on this task. If you let your attention wander from this, then you might end up losing it all. Suppose you stop focusing on your classes and turn your attention to something else. In that case, your grades will eventually start to suffer. If you continue down this path, you will no longer be in college. This can be applied to future job opportunities as well as future relationships. If you start to lose attention to those things, you might end up losing them altogether. You will have to learn how to balance your attention on multiple items, but you will get the hang of it with practice. Remember not to get too distracted by momentary pleasures, rather continue on the path your heart has set you on. It might not be as fun now, but you will be glad you did in the end.

December 15th

"Be wiser than other people, if you can; but do not tell them so."

- Lord Chesterfield: 18th Century British Statesman

No one likes a know-it-all. It is okay to become a know-it-all if you do not become the bad version. The bad version is the stereotypical know-it-all, the one person who has to correct you on everything you say. They are always talking, and when someone chimes in, they shoot them down by telling them how they are wrong. This is not a good person to be because you will lose a lot of friends. The good type is the person who is always seeking out more knowledge. The person who is always reading and always learning. You can never be too smart, and this person embodies that philosophy. They are awesome to have around because you can go to them with any question about anything, and they will have an answer for you. They are very wise, so they know the best way to answer your question to fully understand it. This is a person you can strive to be. The bad know-it-all is someone you should not desire to be, however the good one is a better option for you to strive to become.

December 16th

"When someone is properly grounded in life, they shouldn't have to look outside themselves for approval."

- Epictetus: Ancient Greek Philosopher

Today it is so hard to not look to others for approval. Not only is social media's presence in your life at an all-time high, but you are in a new environment at college. You are probably looking for at least some people to like you. To get to know people and become friends, you will, at some level, have to meet their approval. This approval may not be super high or even noticeable to the person, but it is there. Suppose you go around trying to get everyone's support on who you are as a person. In that case, you will never have any time to get the approval of the most important person in your life...you. Before seeing if you meet others' approval, take a second to see if you meet your own approval. If you do not approve of yourself, why do you think others should approve of you? Once you realize that you are a pretty cool person, you start to realize that you do not need everyone else's approval.

December 17th

"You could leave life right now. Let that determine what you do and say and think."

- *Marcus Aurelius: Roman Emperor & Stoic Philosopher*

Many times, people overcomplicate what it takes to be successful. They will say that you have to do all these different things to succeed. While these pieces of advice have some truth to them, one piece of advice is arguably the most important. If you want success, you have to work for it. That is, you will have success if you just work. All these other pieces of advice are helpful, but you first have to work hard to complete those other pieces of advice. If you want to succeed in school, you have to show up to class. If you want to be successful at your jobs, hobbies, and relationships, you have to work. There are very few people who never worked for anything important to them and somehow became successful. Most of what you need to know to be successful will be found when you show up and work on it. It is not that hard to do; just put your head down and work and you will see success.

December 18th

"Opportunity is missed by most people because it is dressed in overalls and looks like work."
- Thomas Edison 19th Century American Inventor

Unfortunately, many people think that opportunity will just happen to stumble upon them. While this sometimes happens, you have to do some things to have it come looking for you. Opportunity does not just fall at your doorstep one day for no reason. You have to go out and work for it. If you have a goal that you want to accomplish, you need to start working for it now. Maybe you do not have the means to complete that goal right now, but if you work hard now, that opportunity to accomplish it will appear. It is weird how this happens; it usually occurs when you are so busy working that you almost do not notice it. It is like a reward for the hard work that you have done. Sometimes, opportunities take the form of more work. While this does not seem like a reward, you can think of it as a bridge you had to cross to get one step closer to accomplishing your goals. So, start working hard now, and opportunity will find you.

December 19th

"When the winds of change blow, some people build walls and others build windmills."

- Chinese Proverb

You might be wondering when is a good time to change something in your life. There is always something we can change or get better at. Well, you figured out what you need to change, but when? You might think that you will wait until next week, next month, or this summer. None of these is the correct answer. If you want to change, then you need to start today. The sooner you start, the sooner you can get a routine going. Routines are an important part of making a habit. If you start a habit of making yourself better, you are more likely to become better. All too often, you say you will start doing something next week. Time goes by, and all of a sudden, it is next week. This keeps happening, one week at a time. Pretty soon, it has been several months, and you still have not started. The longer you put it off, the less likely you will ever begin. Start today, and you will become more likely to see it through and make a habit of change.

December 20th

"Whatever can happen at any time can happen today."

- Lucius Annaeus Seneca: Roman Stoic Philosopher

A great thing about moving off to college or just even being on your own for the first time is the amount of freedom that you finally have. There is no one looking after you full time anymore, and you can go do everything you have wanted to do. Some of your goals might not be something that can be obtained in one day. Maybe you want to get a college degree or start your own business. These things cannot be done in a day; however, you have to start today if you're going to do it. These tasks might seem daunting at first, but if you keep putting them off, then you will never complete them. The longer you put something off, the harder it becomes to start. You do not want to look back with regret on something you wish you had done. Usually, there is no point in waiting to start something until later. Break these goals of yours down into daily actions, and you will see how gettable these goals will now become. If you truly see yourself obtaining these goals, you have to start at some point. What better time to start chipping away at your goals than today?

December 21st

"Excellence is not a gift, but a skill that takes practice. We do not act rightly because we are excellent in fact we achieve excellence by acting rightly."

- Plato: Ancient Greek Philosopher

People often wonder what it takes to be excellent at something. They think that excellence is tied to something, like being excellent at basketball or math. You might think that you are predestined to be great at something. This is wrong because you can be excellent at anything if you put enough time and energy into it. Excellence is something that is a mindset. If you have an attitude of excellence, then you will be excellent. This is because when you think you can do something, you are more likely to do it in reality. If you have the attitude of excellence, then you are more likely to go about your day doing things that will propel you to be excellent. This attitude makes it easier to do everything necessary to become exceptional. If you do not have the mindset of excellence, then you will be less likely to do this work. So, if you want to be excellent, start having an attitude of excellence.

December 22nd

"Procrastination is the thief of time."
- Edward Young: 18th Century English Poet

It can be quiet jolting to look at the amount of stuff you have to accomplish in one week. Between papers, projects, tests, quizzes, meetings, and work, it can quickly make your head spin. When we are overwhelmed with tasks we need to accomplish, we often procrastinate what needs to be done because it is too much to think about. You might tell yourself the famous lie about how you will feel more energized to accomplish those tasks later. What happens most of the time is that you do not feel energized to accomplish those tasks and you push them off for a longer period of time. How much fun is it to have that giant cloud of obligations you have to complete hanging out in front of you? It would make more sense to start working on everything that you have to do now and finish it. That way, you can go have fun and really enjoy yourself later, without the anxiety of the large tasks that need to be completed. If you want to enjoy your free time later, you should stop putting everything off and start working on it now.

December 23rd

"Wealth is the slave of the wise. The master of the fool."
- Lucius Annaeus Seneca: Roman Stoic Philosopher

People in their twenties find it hard to know what to do with their money. College is the first time you buy a lot of your own necessities. You also have the freedom to spend your money on what you want, without judgment from anyone else. That being said, you really should be cognizant of what you spend your money on. This is not to say that you have to hoard your cash and never spend it on anything fun. Just be mindful of how much you spend, and do not overspend on things you do not really need. The worst thing to do is realize you spent too much money on your weekend out and do not have enough left to make ends meet for the week ahead. If you spend so much that you have nothing left, you have to find some way to make more money. When you have to go through all of this, money is now what is in control of your life. If you spend just a little time making sure to budget and not spend it all, then you are a master of your money.

December 24th

"Freedom is the will to be responsible to ourselves."
- Friedrich Nietzsche: 19th Century German Philosopher

You have probably been looking forward to college for a while now. You could not wait to get out of your high school classes for more engaging college ones. It was time to move out of your parents' house and their rules and move on to making your own rules. Now you are in college, and you are completely free to do whatever you want when you want. This is often when people get in trouble. With this new freedom, you also have an equal amount of personal responsibility. You have the freedom to choose when you go to class, but you have to be responsible enough to not flunk out of college. This means that you have to show up to at least enough of your classes and do enough work to not fail. You have a room completely to yourself, but now you also have the responsibility of keeping it clean and keeping food in the fridge. People are often so excited about this new freedom that they do not realize how much responsibility comes with it. This is just a heads up on what to expect.

December 25th

"Dwell on the beauty of life. Watch the stars and see yourself running with them."

- Marcus Aurelius: Roman Emperor & Stoic Philosopher

When you get to college, you get so busy learning new concepts and meeting new people that you rarely take the time to stop and take it all in. Life is filled with beautiful things every single day, yet we rarely take time to acknowledge these things. Each individual star seems very small to us from the earth, yet all the stars together in the sky paint a beautiful abstract picture in the night sky. The same can be said for the little beauties that occur in your day-to-day life. Alone, they do not seem like much, but when you think of all the beauty in life you have seen that day, it makes a beautiful picture. Every moment of life has a touch of beauty, much like the brilliance of paint on a painting. Take the time to acknowledge these small occurrences in your everyday life. You would be amazed how much it helps you stay positive and learn to really enjoy everything life has to offer. How often do you dwell on life's beauty?

December 26th

"Just as a snake sheds its skin, we must shed our past over and over again."

- Buddha: Ancient Indian Religious Leader

It is never good to let the past keep popping back to the present in your life. We change what we like and dislike; this comes with maturity and wisdom. What you wanted as a freshman in high school will not be the same as what you like when you are a freshman in college. It is good to leave the past in the past and not let it haunt you now. We are all human; we all make mistakes. If you made a mistake in the past, learn the lesson from it but keep it in the past. If it keeps making a presence in the present, then it will affect your stress levels, your happiness, and the decisions on your future. When you let go of the past, you become totally free. You are basically a new person who is free to choose the new things and activities they like. Sure, some things in the past were nice, maybe good friends or a significant other. We often look to the past and only see the good and never think of the bad. Your past was not as good as you think it was; you have much better days ahead of you. Be free of your history, so you can look forward to your future.

December 27th

"Always do the right thing. The rest doesn't matter."
- *Marcus Aurelius: Roman Emperor & Stoic Philosopher*

As long as you do what is right, you should be able to live with the consequences. It should not be hard to choose to do right, because doing the right thing often leads to some pretty good results in your favor. The result could be a heartfelt message from the recipient of your good deed. It could even be a reward in the form of a free dinner or money, depending on what you did. All of these make us feel good about doing the right thing. There are other times when the reward might not be such a big payout. Will you not cheat on this assignment even though the professor will not catch you? Are you going to cheat on your significant other even if they would not catch you? Even when the consequence of doing the right thing is heavily outweighed by doing wrong, will you still do what is right? Your intent should always be to do right; the rest is just added benefit. Plus, when you do the right thing, you never have to worry about the consequences of doing bad.

December 28th

"It may seem difficult at first, but everything is difficult at first."

- *Miyamoto Musashi: 17th Century Japanese Philosopher*

Something that not many new college students realize is when college actually starts. You will arrive at your college, and the first week is basically all fun and parties. Classes have not officially started, so you have all day to do whatever fun things you want to. You might think to yourself that college is going to be a breeze. The first week of classes starts, and all you do is talk about the syllabus and a little class material. No way college is this easy, right? Well, after these first few weeks is when college really starts. The fast pace and difficult material, along with the ever-looming exams, are going to hit you really quickly. This is your first semester of college, and you are struggling. It will be difficult getting adjusted to not only the class portion of college but also the social portion. No other first-semester college student has it together either; they just might be better at hiding it. You will quickly figure out how to study and get to class on time and maintain a social life. It is not worth worrying about because no one gets it at first.

December 29th

"Continuous improvement is better than delayed perfection."

- Mark Twain: 19th Century American Writer

You will notice that you are not going to get everything done at once with many things in college. You will have some long papers that you will need to complete. You are far less likely to achieve it and do it well if you try to do it all at once. Rather, you should break it down into smaller, more manageable sections. Writing a little bit at a time will end up being a better, more thorough paper than if you tried to cram it all at once. The same thing could be said for your college career. You are not going to start and finish college in one day. It will take time to complete. Make a little bit of progress toward achieving your degree. You will see yourself graduating and getting your college degree. Plus, it is mentally more manageable if you can break things down into smaller tasks. If you think about completing college as an enormous task, it can be very overwhelming to think about. If you break down your goals, maybe by semester, into small, obtainable tasks, you will have an easier, less stressful time fulfilling them.

December 30th

"You will find no one willing to share out his money, but to how many does each of us divide up his life."

- Lucius Annaeus Seneca: Roman Stoic Philosopher

Money is not something you will give out to anyone who asks, especially in college. For the first time, you are probably buying most of your necessities. You do not just have a pile of spare money to hand out to others who ask for it. As much fun as it is to spend all your money on things you do not need, it will only lead to issues in the future. The same can be said with time. We do not have an infinite amount of time in a day to give to every person or organization that asks. We cannot hang out with friends every hour of the day in college. The same can also be said for studying too. With social media being more and more accessible, how many hours of the day do you spend looking at that? We divide our day up to many different things, but we rarely think about how important they are. Is what you are giving your time to worth it, or are you just wasting your time with it? Realizing what is taking away your time and transferring that into something productive now gives you the time to succeed.

December 31st

"At break of day, when you are reluctant to get up, have this thought ready to mind: 'I am getting up for a man's work. Do I still then resent it, if I am going out to do what I was born for, the purpose for which I was brought into the world? Or was I created to wrap myself in blankets and keep warm? But this is more pleasant! Were you then born for pleasure – all for feeling, not for action? Can you not see plants, bird, ants, spiders, bees all doing their own work, each helping in their own way to order the world? And then you do not want to do the work of a human being – you do not hurry to the demands of your own nature! But one needs rest too! One does indeed: I agree. But nature has set limits to this too, just as it has to eating and drinking, and yet you go beyond these limits, beyond what you need. Not in your actions, thought, not any longer: here you stay below your capability."

- Marcus Aurelius: Roman Emperor & Stoic Philosopher

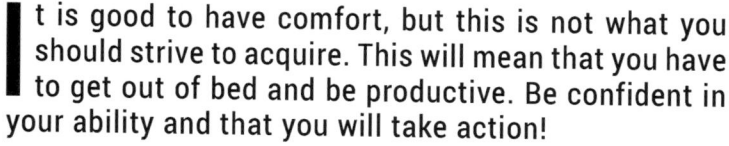

It is good to have comfort, but this is not what you should strive to acquire. This will mean that you have to get out of bed and be productive. Be confident in your ability and that you will take action!

FINAL NOTES

Well, there ya go. You officially made it through this book. I hope that you were able to take a few lessons and ideas away from this book. The great thing about what you learn in here is that you can continue to perfect it for years to come. You can always continue to improve yourself in all aspects. I have a firm belief that all of you will find success. Whether it is now or in the future, I hope that this book helped you to realize your potential, and you will not let it go to waste. Go out and continue the grind towards your dreams. Always remember that you can come back to this book whenever you need a few sentences of motivation. There is no time limit on when you can and cannot put these wise words into effect in your life. You will go through ups and downs, so take what you learned here and apply it wherever it best fits in your life. Again, I wish you all the best and hope you find the successes that you are after.

Best,
Ryan

It Do Be Like That Sometimes

Made in the USA
Middletown, DE
05 September 2022